Culinary Crafting

Culinary Crafting

The Art of Garnishing and Decorating Food

Doris McFerran Townsend

Illustrations by Joan Blume

Rutledge Books
New York
1976

Published in 1976 by Rutledge Books,
25 West 43 Street, New York, N.Y. 10036.
Copyright © 1976 by Rutledge Books,
a division of Arcata Consumer Products
Corporation. All rights reserved.
Printed in the United States of America.
Distributed by Charles Scribner's Sons,
New York, N.Y.

Library of Congress Catalog Card Number: 76-9649
ISBN: 0-87469-002-1

Contents

Introduction

Garnishing and Decorating as a Craft

In the past few years, crafts have taken—quite understandably—an important place in the daily scheme of things for a great many of us. We've learned to create, to work with our hands, and have experienced the intense satisfaction that such accomplishment brings. The piece of needlepoint or bargello that turns into a cushion, a chair seat, a wall hanging; the quilt whose every small stitch was taken with love; the constructions, the paper sculptures, the knitting, crocheting, weaving projects—all of them give us pleasure in the making, in the using, in the giving as gifts.

Cooking, too, is a craft, and making food as pleasing to the eye as to the taste is the ultimate refinement of the craft. The creation of attractive garnishes and decorations can bring satisfaction as great as that gained from any other skill.

As with any handwork, real interest is the foundation. If you are the kind of home cook whose chief object at mealtime is to get something—anything—on the table, the food eaten, and the dishes washed so that you can return to your macramé, you aren't going to be much taken with the idea of exerting effort to make the meal appeal to the eye as well as to the appetite. Because for you food doesn't have much sensual effect, you will see no reason why it should for others.

"Cook" is an honorable appellation; those to whom cooking is creative, who take pleasure in their creations, respond to it proudly. The woman who approaches the making of a meal with anticipation, who takes joy in the shape and color and odor and texture of food as well as the taste, who prides herself on setting an attractive table, who is pleased by compliments and likes to share recipes, responds eagerly to the idea of learning to garnish and decorate with skillful ease and beautiful results.

Is there a difference between garnishing and decorating? Not really. Convention has it that the trimmings added to savory foods are garnishes, the dress-ups for sweet foods are decorations. Whatever they are called, they are like a ribbon in a little girl's hair, a handsome pin on a woman's collar, a bright scarf at the open neck of a man's shirt—none of these is necessary, but each adds a little something that appeals to the senses.

As with virtually everything else, common sense is the best possible starting point for this kind of creativity. A good cook understands seasoning to make foods gratifying to the palate; garnishing and decorating are the seasoning that makes foods satisfying to the eye as well. Pale

Opposite: Savories—pâté and melon basket—and sweets—Spanish Windtorte and tiny tarts

7

meals need color; soft meals need crunch; bland meals need sharpness. *Contrast* and *complement* are the two key words. Common sense.

The cook who wants her productions to look as good as they taste (the reverse needs to be true, as well) learns to think color, texture, size, shape when she makes her shopping list. In planning a meal, she tries to enhance, but never to hide, the beauty of the food itself.

Before it goes to the table, she asks herself, "How does it look?" as an adjunct to "How does it taste?" She considers the lone slice of bacon not as a useless leftover, but as just what's needed to dress up tonight's peas. She takes the necessary extra moment to cut a lemon into wedges and dip the edges in paprika or chopped parsley to grace the veal cutlet. She freezes leftover whipped cream in neat little mounds with some future dessert in mind. She devotes a morning now and then to making little pâte à chou puffs or tiny almond macaroons to freeze, so that they will be on hand when she needs them. When the herb garden yields fresh parsley, dill, basil, or chives, she chops and packages them for the freezer, as insurance against the winter days when the garden offers nothing.

Garnishes and decorations should be edible. The few exceptions are some of the fresh flowers and fresh leaves—but no plastic posies, please, no "Happy Birthday, Bob," worked out in cement. More, not only should such ornamentations be edible, they should also be delicious. They should add a new dimension to the food, to the whole meal. Instead of just sitting there, to be pushed aside as the diner eats, they should be fallen upon with delight.

A garnish, however, should never mask the flavor of the food. And certainly it should never be relied upon to make a bad dish good (although sometimes a substantial garnish can be a lifesaver when the cook's best intentions have produced something less than a masterpiece, as happens to everyone once in a while). Nor should the garnish overpower the food. If the main dish is leg of lamb, it shouldn't come to the table cowering under a whole bed of mint. The cookies should be discernible under the frosting. The cake shouldn't look as if it had been hit by a florist's truck on the way in from the kitchen. Common sense—again, the better part of decorating. "If some is good, more is better," is seldom a useful guide in garnishing.

In this book there are recipes for some foods not usually found in a general cookbook, plus a wealth of information. For the less than deft, there are many easy garnishes and decorations. For the venturesome, there are ideas to spark new ideas. For the clever-handed, there are some more complicated procedures that will be a challenge. There's something for the cook who wants to make ordinary food attractive, the cook who wants to make handsome food even more pleasing to the eye. Something for the novice, for the knowledgeable. For everyone, pleasure and satisfaction. Enjoy.

Savory Garnishes

There are several schools of thought among those who have never given any particular consideration to garnishing the good food they send to the table. Large numbers of these cooks—even those across whose minds the word *garnish* has never strayed—are parsley pushers: a sprig or two to dress up the before-dinner cheese tray, a little bit chopped to float on the soup, a bed of it to cushion the leg of lamb, a drift to disguise the nakedness of the boiled potatoes or to cheer the creamed onions, a sprinkle to enliven the wedge-of-lettuce salad with roquefort dressing. For these cooks, the rain of parsley stops short only at the edge of the ice cream dish and the rim of the coffee cup (this is the dessert area, where whipped cream and maraschino cherries take over).

A second school varies the parsley from time to time with a wedge of lemon, or even combines the two. The venturesome substitute watercress for parsley now and then. The truly revolutionary remember reading somewhere that dill goes very well with fish, and promise themselves to try it on some future occasion. But those small frills are, to many women —even to those who are very good cooks—the alpha and omega of garnishing.

Decorating food is a craft. As with other crafts, the skills to accomplish it, the ideas to implement it, don't come to the novice in a burst of white light. They need to be learned, studied, and practiced until the point is reached where one idea sparks another. Garnishing is fun. It's satisfying. It pleases the eye of the doer and the beholders. It makes good food more inviting. It engenders compliments, and who among us doesn't enjoy a word of praise, a pat on the back?

If you like to cook, and if you like to do things with your hands, you can combine the two by learning the principles and skills of garnishing— and you'll enjoy it, as you enjoy anything else you learn to do expertly, anything else that produces handsome results.

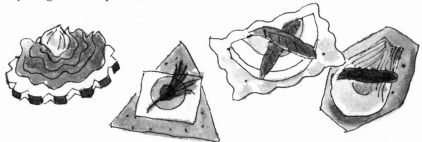

Garnishing Appetizers

A great many appetizers are intrinsically pretty, and in many cases, the inherent garnish is what makes the appetizer taste good. In other words, main-dish garnishes are often solely "for pretty," but appetizer dress-ups usually become, if they are not absolutely necessary, as important to the

Opposite: Stuffed appetizers—baby beets, cherry tomatoes, mushrooms, endive, and dill pickle

flavor of the food as they are to its appearance. A flaky cracker spread with sharp cheese is a reasonably tasty canapé, but when the cheese is topped with a rolled anchovy, a smoked oyster or clam, a tiny cornichon, or even something as simple as concentric small rings of red onion with a few capers, both flavor and looks cheer up at once.

Fine foundations

That which garnishes—and, in the case of appetizers, becomes a part of the goodness—doesn't necessarily have to sit on top of, or even beside, the food being garnished. Canapés, for instance, must have something to sit *on*, and that need not always be a cracker or a slice of party rye. If you like the idea of keeping down calories, slices of raw vegetables—cucumber, zucchini, turnip, rutabaga, carrot, mushroom, radish—make good and good-tasting foundations.

Crackers are good, but sautéed bread is better—cut shapes from thin white or wholegrain bread slices freehand or with a cookie cutter, and sauté them briefly in melted butter until they are lightly browned; they may also be made ahead of time, drained on paper towels, and briefly reheated in a 400° F. oven.

Dense dark bread—all the various "black" breads—are particularly good as foundations for sharp-flavored foods, smoked fish, and smoky cheese; cut the bread in shapes or simply quarter the slices, top them with fish or cheese, and add an appropriate garnish—one that won't be lost in the strong flavor—such as a wedge of gherkin, a slice of radish, or a frill of scallion.

Don't downgrade crackers entirely, though. They have shapes as well as flavors, and those shapes can be used as built-in garnishes. The old standby, cheese and crackers, takes on new interest if the cheese is camembert cut into wedges and arranged in a ring on grape leaves alternately with stacks of triangular crackers. As a finishing touch, place a small bunch of grapes in the center, where the points of the cheese wedges and cracker triangles converge.

Stuff something

Savory mixtures profit by being served in decorative vegetable holders rather than on bread or crackers. Blades of belgian endive, whole inner ribs or chunks of larger ribs of celery or of fennel, raw mushroom caps, hollowed-out cherry tomatoes, little cups made of beets or carrots or zucchini (raw or cooked)—all serve well to hold smooth fillings, bland or sharp, and to add flavor and texture. For cooked vegetables, choose small beets, leaving them whole, and cut 2-inch-long chunks from unpeeled zucchini or scraped carrots; cook them separately in boiling salted water only until they are tender. Use a ball cutter or a sharp, pointed knife to make a hollow for the filling, being sure to leave sufficient vegetable, bottom and sides, so that the cups won't fall apart.

Tuck a whole almond or a tiny pickled onion into the top of the filling, or sprinkle chopped peanuts, walnuts, pecans, or pistachios, snipped chives or mint, or chopped capers on stuffed celery or endive, and you've added another dimension of appeal to both sight and taste.

Dill pickles are very good additions to a tray of appetizers, but, face it, a dill pickle is rather homely, and cutting it into slices or wedges doesn't improve it perceptibly. Ah, but hollow it (use an apple corer), stuff it with a mixture of cream cheese and tiny bits of smoked salmon, chill it thoroughly, cut it into ¼-inch-thick slices, and you have a garnish worth looking at—and worth eating.

Pâté ploys

If you make a delicious pâté for a party, your guests are going to know that you care. If you garnish it so that it ravishes the eyes as well as the taste buds, they're going to know you care a whole lot. Happily, the time and effort required are minimal.

Decorated pâté: In the bottom of a mold that will hold an uncooked, pale-colored pâté, such as one made of salmon or tuna, set a picture-pretty garnish in aspic. When you turn out the pâté, the garnish will be on top. Start by lightly oiling a rectangular mold or loaf pan. Put it into the refrigerator to chill. In a small saucepan, place 1¾ cups cold water and 1 tablespoon unflavored gelatin; let it stand until the gelatin is softened. Then place it over medium heat and stir it until the gelatin is dissolved. Add 1½ teaspoons chicken bouillon powder—the clear kind, without flecks of parsley in it. Stir the mixture until the bouillon is completely dissolved. Pour ½ cup of this gelatin into the loaf pan and return the pan to the refrigerator until the gelatin is firm. Wash and carefully dry three large sprigs of fresh dill. Peel and grate one large carrot. Remove the pan from the refrigerator and gently lay alternating stripes of tiny dill sprigs and grated carrot crosswise on the gelatin layer, letting some gelatin show through between the strips. Press down gently. Place the pan on the refrigerator shelf and gently spoon 3 tablespoons of the remaining liquid gelatin over the top of the garnish. Return the pan to the refrigerator until the gelatin is firm; then spoon the remaining liquid gelatin over the top and chill it again until firm. Now gently pack in the pâté and refrigerate it for 3 hours, or until you are ready to serve it. Unmold the pâté onto a serving platter and surround it with fresh dill sprigs.

The same method will work for almost any kind of garnish-in-aspic that you can think up. Try cutting flowers from very thin crosswise slices of peeled turnip, using a small flower-shaped cookie cutter; use parsley, dill, or watercress for greenery and bits of carrot for flower centers. Or design a flower pot of chopped hard-cooked egg white and decorate it with a stripe of pimiento or carrot or scallion top; for its "plant," a stem of parsley topped with foliage or watercress leaves flecked with tiny bits of pimiento or carrot. Or crisscross the surface of the gelatin with thin slivers of scallion top and place a nutmeat (top side down) or three capers, or a tiny radish or carrot flower, cut with a canapé cutter, in each of the resulting diamond-shaped spaces. Let your imagination have free rein.

If you prefer, skip the gelatin entirely. Instead, frost the well-set, unmolded pâté with a cream cheese thinned to spreading consistency with milk or cream and seasoned with onion juice. Then garnish as you like. A salmon pâté made in a ring mold is very handsome with a wreath of salmon caviar on top and with bits of dill or parsley tucked in for color contrast. Stud the surface of a chicken liver pâté with walnut or pecan halves, or coat it liberally with chopped pistachios or with a mixture of chopped parsley and sieved hard-cooked egg yolk; surround the mold with parsley sprigs. Or make a pattern by overlapping rings of red onion and filling the spaces with the parsley–egg yolk mixture. Border the top of a tuna pâté with thin half-slices of lemon, dipping the cut edge of each slice in paprika before putting it in place, and sprinkle the center with capers.

If you are making a cooked pâté baked in a crust—a glamorous pâté en croûte—gather up and reroll the pastry scraps and cut them (freehand, or make a cardboard pattern to follow) into leaf shapes. Attach the shapes to the top crust with egg yolk diluted with a little cold water. For a handsome golden-brown crust, brush the whole crust, including the decorative shapes, with the egg-yolk wash before baking.

Perhaps you'd like to crown your pâté with a puff-paste crust, deluding your guests into thinking that you labored long and hard. Thaw (in the refrigerator) a package of frozen patty shells. After they've thawed, place them close together on a lightly floured board and roll them out— voilà, a puff-paste crust that would have taken hours had you made it from scratch. Again, reroll the scraps and use them to fancy the top of the crust; bake according to your recipe's directions.

If you are making a baked pâté without a crust, you'll probably produce something savory and delicious but not particularly comely. If you give it a jacket of a wine aspic and top it off with an eye-catching garnish, you will produce something truly spectacular in both taste and looks. Madeira is especially good in a wine aspic for pâtés; follow a recipe in a good general cookbook. No more than two days before the pâté is to be served, remove it from its mold and wipe off any fat and juices on it. Wash and dry the mold and return the pâté to it. Pour in the aspic, reserving several tablespoons to cover the pâté. Chill the pâté until the aspic is set and let the reserved aspic cool at room temperature. Dip appropriate garnishes (orange slices or mandarin orange sections and blades of fresh tarragon would be fine with a duck pâté, for instance; green asparagus tips and quartered slices of lemon would suit a chicken pâté well; halves of tiny pickled ears of corn from a jar is a perfect complement to a pork pâté) into the cool liquid aspic and lay them in place on the set aspic. Chill the pâté until it is firm, and then spoon the remaining liquid aspic gently over the top.

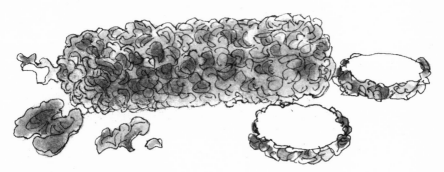

The simple roll-it, sprinkle-it ways

Cheese balls or cheese logs and dips of all kinds are good easy-do make-ahead appetizers. Dressed up a bit, they look extra-fine, too. Roll cheese balls or logs in chopped nuts, in chopped chives, or in chopped parsley, watercress, or dill. In a pinch, with nothing else on hand, roll the cheese ball in paprika for a blaze of color. A pale-hued dip of the cream cheese, sour cream, clam, or horseradish variety profits from a sprinkling of thinly sliced scallions, including plenty of the green tops. A dip for crûdités (raw vegetables) takes kindly to a sprinkling of crushed potato or corn chips or canned french-fried onions. A dip intended for fruit is improved by topping it with chopped filberts or macadamia nuts, slivered ripe olives, or a drift of grated lemon, orange, or lime peel.

High marks in composition

If you are going to serve individual appetizers, which require individual plates for serving and a fork with which to tackle them, or if you plan to offer a platter of raw vegetables with a dip, give a few moments' thought to the composition of the food on the plate. All over the country at dinner time tonight, dabs of chopped chicken liver—very good, but not all that pretty—will be coming to the table. If the diners are lucky, the chicken liver will be seated in cups of boston or bibb lettuce, or spooned into blades of belgian endive or onto a thick tomato slice, or nested in chicory. Or they will have accompanying mounds of chopped onion, or be graced with onion rings. They'll have a little chopped hard-cooked egg, both white and yolk, over them, or a coronet of halved filberts or whole pista-chios, or a cross of pimiento slivers, or a slice cut from a large fresh mushroom. Or they will share the plate with chilled asparagus tips or scallions or green beans vinaigrette—yesterday's leftovers turned into today's delights.

Other such plate-and-fork appetizers can be beautifully composed. Suppose you plan to serve braised leeks with shrimp. Choose a round platter or tray and lay on it, spoke fashion, as many large romaine leaves as there will be servings. Place the braised leeks lengthwise on the romaine and top them with the cooked shrimp—large ones in overlapping rows or small ones spooned over—and sprinkle the shrimp with capers or feathery snipped dill. Place deviled-egg halves between the romaine leaves, and center the platter with a bowl of golden mustard mayonnaise, made by combining 1 teaspoon of dijon-style mustard with each ½ cup of mayon-naise, plus a few drops of lemon juice. Provide a serving fork and spoon, small plates and forks, and let each guest help himself.

Compose a giant canapé—or three or four, depending on the number of guests—using horizontal slices, about ¼ inch thick, from large, round loaves of bread as the base. Spread the slices lightly with butter creamed with a little onion juice. Mound caviar, black or red, in the center. Sur-round the caviar with concentric circles of chopped hard-cooked egg white, chopped scallions, sieved hard-cooked egg yolk, and slices of drained pickled beets. Finish the edge with softened cream cheese flavored gently with horseradish, piped or neatly spooned on. Stick tiny sprigs of parsley into the cream cheese. Try using the same canapé base with concentric circles of julienned rare roast beef, pickled onions, well-drained sauerkraut sprinkled with caraway seeds, thin carrot slices marinated in a sharp vinaigrette, and the horseradish-flavored cream cheese for a border. Or use smoked salmon, chopped scallions, egg white and yolk, cooked frenched green beans vinaigrette, halves of baby pickled eggplants or okra (from a jar), and a border of lemon mayonnaise with dill. Whatever combination you choose, cut the giant canapé in wedges to serve.

Compose a platter of crûdités, keeping in mind color, texture, and taste, and set a bowl of accompanying dip on the platter or close by. Divide a round wooden tray into wedge-shaped sixths with whole scallions. In each of the spaces between, heap sliced raw cauliflower, sliced radishes, carrot strips, cucumber fingers with the peel left on, zucchini rounds, and strips of white turnip. Or compose the vegetables—any combination you like—in concentric circles around the bowl of dip, or put the dip to one side of the platter or tray and arrange the vegetables in diagonal strips. Raw vegetables may also be cut and shaped to be served on their own or to be used as a garnish for other appetizers—see the Garnishing Salads section for such vegetable "sculptures." Dress up small pickles this way: Using a sharp knife, cut them into thin lengthwise slices, starting ⅛ of an inch from the stem end; then gently spread the slices apart to form a fan.

Whatever you choose to offer as an appetizer, there is a way—usually several ways—to dress it up. Garnishing takes only a moment of planning when you decide on your menu, a few moments of doing before you serve.

Garnishing Beverages

A cool drink on a hot day, a warming one when the weather is brisk, a milk drink to turn a sandwich lunch into a hearty meal, a tart one to tease the appetite before dinner, an ice cream concoction that everyone will dote on—all are appealing, all can be made more so by the addition of a delicious garnish and by using a glass that has been appropriately prepared.

The citrus beauties

Lemons, limes, and oranges are all at home with beverages—their juices go into the drink and they can be used in a dozen ways to garnish it. A twist of peel is a perfect cocktail garnish and will also perk up a predinner glass of tomato juice for those who don't want cocktails. When you use a twist, really twist it before you slip it into the drink; the oils in the peel are released, imparting a keen flavor and a delightful aroma.

A citrus slice is the traditional garnish for a tall fruit drink or for iced tea. To make one, cut a ⅛-inch slice of lemon, orange, or lime for each drink. Using a sharp knife, slit the slice from the center through the peel; slip the cut over the rim of the glass. A citrus curl goes the slice one better: Cut the peel at one point and cut away half the fruit pulp from inside the peel; curl the free peel tightly toward the center and perch the slice on the rim of the glass.

If you prefer, garnish a beverage with a wedge of citrus fruit that can be squeezed into the drink. It, too, can be placed on the rim of the glass— cut a small slit in the center of the wedge. It will be twice as pretty, twice as good, if you dip the center of the wedge into chopped mint or parsley or into ground spice. Peach nectar, for example, is improved by a lemon wedge dipped in nutmeg. Dip the wedge in mace to perk up old-fashioned orangeade, in cinnamon to give new flavor to iced tea, into pepper or garlic powder for tomato or mixed-vegetable juice. For a change, stud the lemon wedge with three or four whole cloves.

Stirrers, swizzlers, kabobs

For these you'll need food picks, thin bamboo skewers—stocked with the oriental foods in your supermarket—and ice cream pop sticks. To make a citrus swizzle stick, cut a ¼-inch slice of fruit, make a slit in the peel, and insert an ice cream stick so that the whole thing looks like a lollipop. Place the swizzle stick in the freezer for an hour or so, and then plunk it into the drink. For a smaller drink, quarter lemon or orange slices and thread two of the pieces, points together, onto a food pick. Another version for a small drink is to cut lime slices in half and thread the halves at right angles to one another on a food pick. For color contrast, add a cranberry or a cherry. These can be frozen if you like, refrigerated for up to 3 hours, or used when freshly made.

As a garnish for a cold summer fruit drink that refreshes eye, taste, and spirit, make fruit kabobs: Thread pineapple chunks, whole berries, grapes or kumquats, sections of mandarin orange or fresh orange, lemon, or lime, maraschino or pitted fresh cherries, melon balls, or bite-size pieces of any kind of fruit, on thin bamboo skewers. In making these, try for shape and color contrast. Thread mint leaves between the fruit pieces for both looks and flavor. Chunks of watermelon pickle, pickled canta-

Opposite: Limeade with fruit kabobs and lime slices

loupe, or any sort of brandied fruit make delightful surprise-taste additions to these kabobs.

Ice dresses up to go to a party

Punch to be served from a punch bowl needs a large piece of ice to cool it, for cubes melt rapidly and dilute the punch too much and too soon. Almost all cold drinks need ice cubes; some of them require shaved ice. There's no reason that all this ice can't be good-looking, that it can't be flavorful, too, so that when it melts it won't dilute the drink it's cooling.

To make an ice block for the punch bowl, fill a ring mold, metal mixing bowl, or loaf pan halfway with water or with fruit juice or with whatever base you are using for the punch. (Remember that alcohol doesn't freeze—add it later—and that carbonated beverages will lose their fizz if frozen.) Put the container into the freezer until the liquid is partially frozen. Arrange fruit pieces—whatever kind will complement the punch, or a mixture of several kinds—on the ice. Arrange mint sprigs, nasturtium leaves, or small grape leaves in decorative patterns around the fruit. Return the container to the freezer until the garnish is well frozen and fixed in place. Gently fill the container with very cold water or juice and freeze the ice solid.

Work the same way on a smaller scale for decorative ice cubes, using pieces of fruit and leaves, a twist or curl of citrus peel, a shape cut from citrus peel or, for nonsweet drinks, from thin slices of vegetables such as a carrot or turnip, or a curl of cucumber peel. Fill the ice cube trays halfway, partially freeze the water, position the garnish and freeze the water completely, fill the trays, and freeze the ice until firm.

For iced tea, make cubes of a lemon juice—water combination and garnish them with pieces of lemon, orange, or lime and/or mint leaves, or use slivers of candied ginger. For iced coffee, freeze brewed coffee in the cube tray for a full-bodied drink; that way you can use regular, rather than double-strength, beverage for your iced coffee. Pour coffee into glasses over the coffee cubes and gently float a small amount of heavy cream on top—serve the drink at once, as the cream seeps down into the coffee in a lovely pattern. Use a twist of lemon peel or a clove-studded slice of orange to garnish the glasses of those who don't take cream in their coffee.

Freeze fruit or vegetable juice to make shaved ice. If your kitchen is blessed with an ice crusher, use that; if not, a trip to your hardware store will get you an inexpensive, easy-to-use hand ice shaver.

Milk drinks, ice cream drinks

Don't overlook the childhood joy of experiencing a creamy marshmallow melting in a cup of hot cocoa or a dab of whipped cream slowly blending its coldness with the warmth of a hot drink. Or top a cold chocolate drink with whipped cream, sprinkle the cream with grated orange peel, and add a cinnamon-stick stirrer—it's pleasing to the eye and adds great flavor.

Add a new dimension to Orange Velvet—made by whirling equal parts of frozen orange juice concentrate and vanilla ice cream in the blender—with a sprinkling of nutmeg, or chocolate curls or cutouts (see Index). For a peach drink, cut a juicy wedge of fresh peach, dip it in lemon juice to keep it from darkening, stud it with almond slices, and perch the wedge on the rim of the glass. A strawberry shake takes on glamour when you add a kabob made of strawberries and pineapple chunks. Any milk–fruit drink is at its best when served with a kabob made of the fruit on which the drink is based, plus another fruit for flavor and color contrast.

When you make homemade ice cream sodas—easy, and generally a whole lot better than the ones from the corner drugstore—perch the final ball of ice cream on the rim of the glass rather than dropping it into the drink. Sprinkle it with something both good-tasting and pretty—chopped nuts, grated chocolate, spice, grated citrus peel, or coarse colored sugar. Or top the soda with sweetened, flavored whipped cream, add whatever sprinkle you like, and/or crown it with a cherry.

The glasses are part of the picture

Chill glasses for drinks—never chill wine glasses—in the refrigerator or freezer until they are cold and frosty. Or frost the glasses this way: Dip the rims in slightly beaten egg white, or in citrus fruit juice, or even in water, and then dip them into sugar—white or colored—or, for nonsweet drinks, into salt. You can sugar them as heavily as like, but go easy on the salt. The egg-white treatment stands up longer than the others, but it is harder to wash off. If you want to frost glasses in advance, refrigerate them until serving time.

Whether the motive is thirst or sociability, everyone looks forward to a good drink. If the beverage is both tasty and attractive there's never a disappointed imbiber.

Garnishing Soups

Beautiful soup, that most versatile of dishes! A light soup gets a meal off to a great start. In the event of droppers-in at mealtime, a well-garnished bowl of soup can extend dinner for four to dinner for six without letting your panic show. Served with bread and salad, soup can be a meal in itself. Steaming mugs of soup serve as a pick-me-up after outdoor work or play in cold weather. Chilled soup can be a genuine refresher on a hot day, when appetites lag. And as a bonus, soup—both in the making and in the garnishing—can act as the ultimate medium for using up leftovers without anyone but you being the wiser.

Rafts and other beef-it-up additions

It's traditional to garnish onion soup with a thick, lavishly cheesed slice of french bread, the whole thing run under the broiler for a few minutes before serving. Delicious and satisfying, right? What law says that the same idea can't be applied to almost any other soup–bread–topping combination?

Try rye bread with muenster on a vegetable soup that has cabbage as one of its ingredients. Top dark bread with crumbled blue cheese to lighten up a hearty beef broth. Cream cheese on white bread, sprinkled with snipped chives or parsley, finishes a chicken or delicate fish soup to perfection. Good, sharp cheddar on french bread goes well with pea soup; a bit of leftover ham tucked under the cheese turns the soup into a stick-to-your-ribs meal. Sourdough bread with a drift of parmesan or romano complements any hearty fish soup. Now that you've got the idea for composing rafts, try any combination that pleases you.

Will it float?

Cream soups, clear soups, and purées cry out for something to break up their smooth, flat surfaces. Slices of hard-cooked egg and a bit of chopped raw onion are traditional with lentil soup and are so good that there's no reason to break with tradition. Unsweetened whipped cream or dairy sour cream or plain yogurt are delicious on cream of tomato soup; sprinkle the dairy topping with something—chopped parsley or watercress, paprika, chopped peanuts, chili powder, curry powder, turmeric—to relieve the whiteness and add zest. Give pea soup the same treatment. Or garnish pea or bean soup with a slice of fresh tomato sprinkled with basil.

Croutons are just what a smooth, creamy soup needs to give it crunch. You can buy them, plain or flavored, in packages, but you can also make them—cheaper and tastier, as almost all homemade things are.

Plain croutons for a rich soup: Trim the crusts from day-old bread slices and cut the bread into cubes of any size that takes your fancy. Spread the cubes on a baking sheet and toast them in a 375°F. oven for about 15 minutes, or until they are crisp and brown.

Buttered croutons: Butter the bread slices on both sides and proceed as you would to make plain croutons.

Flavored croutons: Toss the cubes cut from four slices of bread in ⅓ cup of French or Italian salad dressing; bake them as you would plain croutons.

Cheese croutons: Use buttered cheese bread to make these. An alternate method is to sprinkle the top sides of buttered croutons with grated parmesan or romano cheese before baking.

Seasoned croutons: Sprinkle buttered croutons with curry powder, chili powder, dried and crumbled basil, oregano, savory, marjoram, or thyme, or grated lemon, orange, or lime peel, or any combination of seasonings that strikes your fancy, before baking.

To add attractive substance to almost any soup, float whatever leftover your refrigerator has to offer on top of the soup. Here are a few ideas to get you started: frenched green beans, slivers of almost any kind of cheese, strips of ham or chicken, cooked pasta, chopped hard-cooked egg, or almost any vegetable. Suit the garnish to the color (contrast with it) and the flavor (complement it) of the soup on hand. Raw vegetables, too, cut in shapes with small cookie or canapé cutters or in julienne strips, are fine soup garnishes. And don't make the mistake of downgrading our old friends, parsley and lemon.

Made with love

Almost every culture that has been a part of the making of America has a soup garnish that is one of its minor contributions. Here are some of them for you to try:

Chinese egg drops: For four servings of soup, beat 2 eggs with 2 tablespoons of water. Pour the mixture gradually into boiling chicken or beef broth, stirring as you pour. Cook for 1 minute.

Greek avgolemono: To four servings of chicken broth, add 2 tablespoons of lemon juice and 1 cup of cooked rice. Heat the mixture until boiling, and then add egg drops as you would for Chinese egg drops. Sprinkle the soup with chopped parsley.

Austrian wiener erbsen: Heat fat to 375°F. in a deep fryer. Sift together ¾ cup of all-purpose flour and ¼ teaspoon salt and reserve. Beat together 1 egg and 2 tablespoons of milk; add the mixture all at once to a well in the center of the dry ingredients. Beat the batter until it is smooth and well blended. Drop it into hot fat by ¼ teaspoons and fry the dumplings for 1 to 2 minutes, until they are golden. Remove the dumplings and drain them on paper towels; float a spoonful of them in each plate of clear soup.

Swedish cheese nuggets: Combine and reserve ⅓ cup of fine dry bread crumbs and ¼ cup of finely shredded sharp cheese. In a small bowl, beat together lightly 1 egg, ¼ teaspoon each of salt and dry mustard, and ⅓ teaspoon of paprika. Blend in the crumbs–cheese mixture to make a thick paste. Drop the mixture by teaspoonfuls into simmering soup and cook for 2 or 3 minutes.

Pennsylvania Dutch rivels: Bring 1 quart of milk to a boil. Combine 1 egg with 1 cup of all-purpose flour. Rub the egg–flour mixture between your hands, letting shreds of it fall into the boiling milk. The boiled milk plus the rivels served alone is Rivel Soup; or you can add the rivels to chicken–corn soup.

Almost any good cookbook will give you recipes for other ethnic soup additions—tiny meatballs (albondigas) for a Mexican-style soup; little sausage balls (drain them well) for an Irish touch; liver dumplings for German-style cooking; matzo balls for a Jewish addition. Make up a recipe of pâte à chou (cream-puff pastry), stir in shredded swiss or grated parmesan cheese, and drop the mixture by rounded teaspoonfuls into boiling salted water until these little Danish dumplings rise to the surface. Or bake the dough as for cream puffs, using only ½ teaspoon for each puff, to make Russian soup nuts.

An elegant-but-easy British soup garnish is this one, a sort of baked omelet.

Royal custard: Beat together lightly 1 egg, ¼ teaspoon of sugar, ⅛ teaspoon each of salt and paprika, and a dash of white pepper. Slowly add ⅓ cup of scalded milk, beating constantly. Strain the mixture into a 5-inch-square baking pan, and set the pan into a larger pan. Pour boiling water into the larger pan, filling it to the level of the egg mixture. Bake at 325°F. until it is set, about 30 minutes. Remove the 5-inch pan from the larger pan and cool the custard. Cut the custard into cubes or any shape you fancy, and slip them into hot consommé just before serving. What do you have? Consommé Royale.

Hot and cold ideas

Sometimes a little of whatever ingredient you have made the soup from is a just-right garnish. Try using two thin slices of scored, unpeeled cucumber on cold cucumber cream, a lengthwise slice of avocado on avocado cream. Shredded raw beets make a beautiful surprise addition to borscht.

A carrot curl or carrot shreds dress cream of carrot; whole spinach leaves float gracefully on cream of spinach; and small, raw celery sticks stuffed into pitted ripe olives make a colorful bonus for cream of celery soup.

Sometimes contrast is called for. On a curried cream soup, hot or cold, float a thin slice of a cored, unpeeled apple—dunk the slice in lemon juice first so that it won't darken. Half a deviled egg is a fine idea for any seafood bisque, or sprinkle such soups with tiny shrimps and snipped chives or parsley or chopped celery leaves.

Popcorn (unbuttered) sits up perkily on the surface of soup and tastes good, too. Raw onion rings or green pepper rings make a pretty, tasty soup garnish. So do canned french-fried onions, chinese noodles, slices of sausage, crumbled bacon, chopped or sliced olives, oyster crackers or cheese crackers, or halved pretzel sticks or a handsome whole large pretzel.

Almost any garnish is a good soup garnish—just bear in mind color and texture contrast and you will have it made.

Garnishing Main Dishes

Instead of a sometime thing, saved until there are guests, garnishing should be a part of every meal for family or for company. You may want to hoard your best efforts for a party, but there's a great deal you can do, without expense of time or effort, to make everyday meals more appealing.

For instance, when you prepare a main dish for the table, place it on a platter or serving dish large enough to hold the vegetables as well— nicely arranged. If you're having pot roast, hot or cold, slice it in the kitchen—a pot roast isn't so pretty that you can't bear not to bring it to the table whole—arrange the slices neatly on the platter with a bowl of gravy in the center or at one end, tuck in a few sprigs of watercress, and there you are. If you're having a cold poached fish and marinated cucumbers, arrange the cucumbers, dill sprinkled, around the fish on the platter, with a bowl of whatever sauce you're serving placed at one end.

Give the family meal a moment's thought, and it will look as good as it tastes. When company's coming, set your sights high and prepare to field with becoming modesty the shower of compliments.

New look for an old friend

Everybody likes potatoes, but they are not things of beauty. They are pale and, for the most part, shapeless. Dress them up a bit, however, and they can be rewarding additions to any meal. Even a bowl of mashed potatoes isn't hopeless. Top the mound with a good-sized pat of butter while the potatoes are hot so that it will melt into enticing rivulets. Sprinkle the colorless white with something to take the curse off—chopped parsley, grated cheese, buttered bread crumbs, or even paprika if there's nothing else at hand.

When you really put your mind to it, you can make the potato part of the meal the glamorous part. Try one of the following variations the next time you serve potatoes to guests.

Golden nests: Peel, boil, and drain 2 pounds of potatoes; put them through a sieve or ricer into a bowl. Stir in 3 tablespoons of butter, 2 egg yolks, and 1 whole egg. Season them to taste with salt, white pepper, and nutmeg. Spoon the mixture into a pastry bag with a large decorative tube; pipe small mounds onto a lightly buttered baking sheet. (If you're not up on pastry tubes, form the mounds with two spoons.) With the back of a spoon, press a small hollow into each mound. Combine 1 egg with 1 tablespoon of cream and brush the mounds with the mixture. Place the mounds under the broiler for 1 or 2 minutes, or until they are lightly browned. Fill the nests with a vegetable—creamed or sautéed mushrooms, buttered peas or asparagus tips, broccoli flowerets—and arrange the nests on a serving platter surrounding the main dish.

Duchess potatoes: Use the potato mixture for making golden nests, above, to pipe a full, continuous border around the chops or steak on a plank. Brush the potatoes with the egg–cream mixture and brown them under the broiler. If you like, fill the space between the potatoes and the meat with another vegetable.

Jackstraw baskets: Shred raw potatoes; wash the shreds well in cold water and drain them thoroughly. Layer the shreds in a sieve; then press another, slightly smaller sieve into the first. Lower the sieves into deep fat, heated to 390°F., and fry the potatoes until they are crisp. Carefully remove the potato basket from the sieves and drain it on paper towels. Repeat until all the potatoes have been used. Keep the baskets warm in the oven; just before serving, fill them with vegetables or with creamed chicken or fish. If you fall in love with these pretty, tasty little baskets, any shop that sells gourmet utensils can provide you with a hinged double-basket device for making them.

Opposite: Vegetable flowers

Uniformity is not a dirty word

When you're preparing vegetables for a special-occasion meal, take the few extra minutes it requires to make them into uniform shapes. Cut potatoes, turnips, or rutabagas into neat balls with the large end of a melon baller, or trim them with a sharp knife into large olive shapes. Cook them until they are barely tender, drain them well, and sauté them briefly in butter. (If you like, add a little sugar to the butter, in the Danish manner, for a browner, tastier glaze.) When you buy asparagus, make sure that the stalks are uniform in diameter; when you prepare it, make sure that they're uniform in length. Use only the flowerets of broccoli. Buy baby carrots, and trim them to uniform size and shape. (Glaze these in butter/sugar—brown or white—if a sweet touch is appropriate to the rest of the meal.) Sauté uniform-size cherry tomatoes briefly for a glowing red color. Any of these shapely vegetables makes an attractive edible border garnish for a platter of meat, fish, or poultry. And you're not being wasteful—cook the trimmings and mash or purée them for another meal, or use them in soup.

The ubiquitous mushroom

There's no middle course with mushrooms—you either love them or hate them. To mushroom lovers, a garnish of sautéed mushrooms, or a big, fluted mushroom cap crowning a chop or filet mignon, or a garland of them around a steak or a roast of beef is a sight to bring tears to the eyes.

Sherry-sautéed mushrooms: Wipe 1 pound of mushrooms clean with a damp cloth. Quarter the large ones through the stems; leave the small ones whole. In a skillet, combine the mushrooms, 2 tablespoons of butter, and ¼ cup of sherry; cover the mushrooms and cook them over high heat for 2 minutes. Uncover them and continue to cook them until the liquid evaporates. Continue to cook them, stirring constantly, over high heat until they are lightly browned. Season them to taste with salt and pepper.

(Mushroom purists may wish to omit the sherry and increase the butter to 3 tablespoons.) One pound of mushrooms makes six garnish servings. If you are serving more people or if you are serving the mushrooms as a vegetable, increase the amounts accordingly.

Fluted mushrooms: Wipe medium-size mushrooms clean with a damp cloth. Cut off the stems even with the caps (save them to make cream of mushroom soup another day). Using a sharp, thin-bladed knife, mark the center of each cap. Starting at the center, make a ⅛-inch-deep curved cut to the edge of the cap. Repeat, making eight evenly spaced cuts around the cap. Make a second cut just behind each of the first eight cuts, slanting the knife toward the first cut. Lift out the resulting narrow strip. Sauté the fluted caps in heated butter—to which a little lemon juice has been added—for 1 to 2 minutes, cap side down, until they are golden; turn the caps and sauté them 1 minute longer.

Mushroom kabobs: On food picks, alternate cooked fluted mushrooms with pitted ripe olives or stuffed green olives or cubes of cooked vegetable. Top the kabob with a pickled onion.

Cups, saucers, and the like

A simple garnishing maxim is this: Put something inside something else. Its corollary: Two is better than one. Vegetables can be used as containers for other vegetables or for relishes; so can fruits. And there are all sorts of other containers into which foods can be heaped for a pleasing—and delicious—effect.

Artichoke bottoms (they come ready to use in cans or jars, or prepare them yourself—any good general cookbook will tell you how) filled with cooked peas, sautéed mushrooms, or almost anything else you want to use to complement your dinner, make an attractive and delectable garnish. Use the artichoke bottoms in multiples on a platter, or one at a time to decorate a single serving. Top an artichoke bottom with a large fluted mushroom and place the pair on a small steak or filet mignon—add béarnaise sauce and you have a beautiful, classic dish. Or fill the bottoms with crab or shrimp to garnish a cold entrée, such as a salmon mousse. Or heat them and fill them with vegetables, or with pea or bean purée, to accompany hot entrées.

Beets, turnips, and carrots make attractive small cups in which to put a sauce or relish. Choose medium-size, uniform beets or turnips, or 2½- to 3-inch sections of large carrots. Peel the turnips and carrots before cooking, the beets afterward. Cook them in boiling salted water until they are barely tender. Using a sharp knife and a small spoon, hollow out the vegetable, and fill it with the sauce or relish you wish to complement your meal. Beet cups are particularly nice to hold the traditional horseradish accompaniment for boiled beef. Large peeled whole onions, cooked until they are barely tender and scooped out, make attractive containers. So do halved sweet peppers, red or green—use raw peppers to hold garnish salads such as cole slaw or marinated vegetables, parboil them for about 5 minutes if they are to contain cooked foods.

Citrus fruits, halved and with the pulp removed, make attractive cups to hold sauces or other garnishes. Plunge a sharp knife into the fruit in a zigzag pattern around the center; pull the fruit apart and hollow it out, using a grapefruit knife and a spoon. You may leave a "handle" of peel in place, turning the shells into baskets. If necessary, cut a thin slice off the bottom of the fruit to make the shell stand without tipping. The shells, with their serrated borders, are then ready to fill. Lemon shells hold tartar or hollandaise sauce to serve with fish or vegetables, or mint jelly for lamb. Orange shells are fine for cranberry sauce or currant jelly or cranberry–orange–walnut relish to serve with poultry, or for cumberland sauce to serve with game. A grapefruit shell can double as a serving dish for plain, flavored, or herbed mayonnaise or for a grapefruit-juice hollandaise or a maltaise sauce. Or for almost anything else you want to use it for.

Patty shells are handsome, and they can serve well to flesh out a meal if there are unexpected additional diners. A word—or three, rather—of advice about patty shells: don't make them. Many good bakeries save you the time and trouble, and there are excellent frozen patty shells on the market, too. Serve sauced mixtures in patty shells—seafood in newburg sauce, creamed sweetbreads, and the old-but-still-good chicken à la king are only three of dozens of possibilities. Serve vegetables in them, too, sauced or not; creamed green vegetables, such as spinach or chard or kale or broccoli or brussels sprouts, are especially good.

Barquettes—pastry in the shape of a boat—serve the same purposes as patty shells. Although they are not large enough to hold a main-dish serving, they can contain any number of savory garnishes or simply be used to hold such vegetables as peas or a pea–mushroom combination. Buy the shells at an elegant bakery, or refer to a good cookbook for a barquette recipe. If you prefer, use the recipe by which you make pie crust, or packaged pie crust mix. Barquette tins—small fluted ovals—can be purchased, or make use of tiny muffin or tartlet pans.

Plain white bread—the old-fashioned, firm-textured kind is best—can be used to make crisp, tasty cases in which to serve creamed or sauced foods. Trim off all the crusts from a loaf of unsliced bread. Cut the loaf into 1½-inch-thick slices, and then round off the points of each slice. Hollow out each slice, leaving a shell about ⅛ inch thick. Spread the shells, both outside and in, with softened butter; place them on baking sheets and bake them at 400°F. for about 12 minutes, or until they are crisp and golden. Or leave the bread unsliced, hollow the entire loaf, and proceed as above to make a big croustade. (Such croustades, filled with fried oysters, were once popular as wife-appeasers—they were brought home in the small hours by husbands who had stayed late at the club, the gaming table, or the local saloon.)

A rice ring serves the same purpose—to add shape and contrast to a creamed or sauced mixture and, at the same time, to supply an added dimension to the meal. Cook the rice (either brown or white) according to package directions. Pack it firmly into a well-buttered ring mold, place the serving plate over the mold, and turn both upside down. Shake them a bit to dislodge the rice ring. If you like, add finely chopped mushrooms, snippets of pimiento or olive, or chopped parsley or watercress to the rice before molding.

New ways with table greenery

Sometimes a bed of greens is just the right garnish for a main dish. A plump roasted chicken, well browned, looks sumptuous on a bed of watercress, with a few pale yellow celery leaves tucked here and there for contrast. Watercress alone, or celery leaves alone, or parsley or nasturtium or grape leaves, or little frills of bibb or butter lettuce—any of these makes a pretty bed for almost any meat, fish, or poultry main dish. If you want color contrast, tuck half-slices of lemon, or wedges of mandarin orange, or whole raw cranberries or cherries, or cherry tomatoes or tiny yellow pear tomatoes, or stuffed or green-ripe olives among the greens. Add a few small bunches of grapes when you use grape leaves and some of the bright blossoms of the plant when you use nasturtium leaves.

There are other things to do with our most-often-used garnish greens that make them appealingly new and different. Try these.

Fried parsley: Wash the parsley sprigs and dry them well. Heat deep fat to 375° F. Fry the parsley sprigs, a few at a time, for just a few seconds —until they begin to get crisp. Drain them on paper towels and sprinkle them with salt.

Parsley fritters: In a bowl, combine ½ cup of sifted all-purpose flour, 1 egg, and 1 egg yolk. Add 3 tablespoons of milk, 1 tablespoon of melted butter, and ¼ teaspoon of salt. Beat the mixture smooth with a rotary beater. Add 3 additional tablespoons of milk and 1 teaspoon of baking powder; mix the batter well. Beat 1 egg white until stiff; fold it into the first mixture. Refrigerate the mixture for 30 minutes. Heat deep fat to 370° F. Wash and dry well 24 sprigs of parsley with long stems. Remove the batter from the refrigerator and beat it well. Hold each sprig by the stem and dredge it in flour; then dip it in the batter, shaking off any excess— the parsley should be thinly coated. Fry two sprigs at a time in the hot fat for only a moment or two, until they are golden. Drain the sprigs on paper towels and sprinkle them with salt.

Watercress fritters: Place 1½ cups of light beer in a mixing bowl. Gradually add about 1 cup of all-purpose flour, blending it well, until you have a batter the consistency of heavy cream. Heat deep fat to 390° F. Wash and dry the watercress sprigs. Holding them by the stems, dip the sprigs into the batter. Drop them into the hot fat and fry them for a few seconds, until they begin to crisp. Drain the fritters on paper towels and sprinkle them with salt.

Crowns and other kingly dishes

A crown roast—of lamb or pork—or a rack of lamb or a standing rib roast of beef is a good choice to serve guests whose tastes you aren't too sure

Opposite: Crown roast of lamb with kumquats, peas and mushrooms in artichoke bottoms

of. French the bones (trim the meat at the ends, leaving the bones bare) or ask the butcher to do it. When you put the meat in the roasting pan, cover the end of each bone with a small piece of aluminum foil to keep it from charring. (If you are stuffing a crown roast, put foil in the center of the well, too, pressing it up the sides, before you pile in the stuffing, so that you can remove the roast from the pan intact.)

When the roast is done, remove it to a heated platter, and take the foil off the bones. There you are, with a handsome roast doing its 20 minutes of standing time before serving so that it will cut well—but with its bare bones hanging out. On pork or lamb, you can't do better than to stick a preserved kumquat on the end of each bone. Surround the pork roast with sautéed fruit of some kind (suggestions are given below). Watercress fritters (see Index) are wonderful with lamb, or surround lamb roasts with fresh mint sprigs and more kumquats. Spear a cherry tomato (or, if the bones are large, a small regular tomato) on each beef bone, and encircle the roast with fluted mushroom caps alternated with broiled tomato halves sprinkled with parmesan cheese.

You can, of course, buy—or make—little french paper "panties" for the ends of the bones. Sometimes the butcher will give them to you when you buy one of these roasts, and so he ought, considering the price. But fruit or vegetable garnishes are prettier, are edible, and eliminate that catered look.

Fruitful ideas

Fruit and meat pair well, and fruit garnishes add a little extra something to a meal from both the good taste and the good looks standpoints.
Sautéed apple rings: Core, but do not peel, large baking apples—rome beauties are good for these—and cut each into four even rings. Sauté them in butter in a single layer over medium heat. Cook them for 5 minutes on each side, or until they are tender and lightly browned. Sprinkle the rings generously with a cinnamon–sugar mixture and serve them warm.
Sautéed bananas: Peel bananas and, unless they are very small, cut them in half crosswise. Sauté them in butter over medium heat until they are golden. Serve the bananas hot, either plain or sprinkled lightly with lemon juice.

Pickled pineapple rings: Drain the syrup from canned pineapple into a saucepan. To the syrup from each 1-pound can, add ¼ cup of cider vinegar and 1 teaspoon of mixed pickling spices. Bring the syrup to a boil; reduce the heat and simmer the syrup for 5 minutes. Strain it over the pineapple slices and refrigerate them. At serving time, roll the edge of each pineapple ring in paprika or chopped parsley. Or you can sauté well-drained pineapple rings (either pickled or from the can) in butter; serve them with a garnish of paprika or chopped parsley.

Quick pickled peaches: Drain the syrup from canned peach halves into a saucepan. To the syrup from each 1-pound can, add ½ cup of white vinegar, three 1-inch pieces of stick cinnamon, 5 whole cloves, ¼ cup of firmly packed brown sugar, and ¼ teaspoon (or 2 blades) of mace. Bring the syrup to a boil; reduce the heat and simmer the syrup for 5 minutes. Strain it over the peaches and refrigerate them. At serving time, drain the peaches and fill the centers of each with a small spoonful of currant or mint jelly.

Almond peaches: Drain the syrup from canned peach halves into a saucepan. Add 2 pieces of stick cinnamon and 3 drops of almond extract to the syrup, and simmer it as above. Strain the syrup over the peaches and refrigerate them. At serving time, drain the peaches and fill the centers with slivered toasted almonds and dribble a few drops of syrup over the almonds.

Brandied peaches or apricots: Drain the syrup from a 1-pound can of fruit into a saucepan. Bring the syrup to a boil; reduce the heat and simmer the syrup until it is reduced by half and thickened, for about 15 minutes. Remove it from the heat. When the syrup is cool, add ¼ cup of brandy. Pour the syrup over the fruit; cover it and refrigerate it for 2 to 3 days. At serving time, drain the fruit and stud each piece with sliced almonds.

Comforted prunes: In a container with a cover, soak a 1-pound box of pitted prunes and the julienned peel of a large orange in enough Southern Comfort liquor to cover the fruit. This concoction should be started at least two weeks before you want to use the prunes. Cover the prunes, but do not refrigerate them. After two weeks, drain off most of the liquor, leaving only enough to keep the prunes moist. The prunes will keep indefinitely at room temperature (but are not likely to last long once you've tried them). At serving time, stuff each prune with a pecan or a walnut or a bit of cream cheese.

Spiced fresh pears: In a large enamel saucepan, combine 2 cups of sugar, 1 cup of cider vinegar, 1 tablespoon of coriander seed, three 2-inch pieces of stick cinnamon, and a 1-inch piece of dried gingerroot. Bring the mixture to a boil over low heat, and simmer it for 5 minutes. Peel, halve, and core 2 pounds of firm-ripe pears; place a few pieces of pear at a time in the syrup and simmer them for 10 to 15 minutes, or until they are tender. Transfer them to a glass or ceramic bowl; cover and refrigerate them. At serving time, give the rounded part of each pear half a blush of paprika.

Mulled-wine pears: Drain the syrup from a 1-pound can of pears; add a 3-inch piece of stick cinnamon, 6 whole cloves, and a 3-inch piece of lemon peel. Stir in 1 cup of red table wine. Bring the mixture to a boil; reduce the heat and simmer the mixture for 5 minutes. Strain it over the pear halves and refrigerate them. At serving time, fill the centers of the fruit with small cream cheese balls that have been rolled in chopped walnuts.

Fruit plays a part in the cooking and garnishing of many main dishes. Look in the index of a good general cookbook for recipes for duck à l'orange or montmorency (with black cherries) or for fish veronique with white grapes), and for many meat–fruit combinations. Browse the shelves of your supermarket or gourmet food shop for readymade fruit garnishes —pickled crabapples, cinnamon apple rings, minted pears and pineapple, brandied peaches, pickled limes, and brandied cherries.

Stuffing makes a dish doubly pretty, doubly good

Stuffed vegetables serve as a savory, attractive garnish to border a main-dish serving platter. Many such garnishes offer the added advantage of providing the vegetable portion of the meal.

Stuffed mushrooms I: Cut off the stems of large mushrooms even with the caps. Sauté the caps briefly in butter to brown the cap side lightly. Place the caps in a baking pan. Chop the stems coarsely and add to them an equal amount of fresh bread crumbs plus ½ teaspoon of chopped almonds, ½ teaspoon of finely minced onion, and ⅛ teaspoon of dried savory for each mushroom. Cook the stuffing in melted butter for 3 minutes; season it to taste with salt and pepper. Pile the stuffing into the mushroom caps and keep the caps warm in the oven until ready to serve. Just before serving, tuck a tiny sprig of parsley into the stuffing on each cap.

Stuffed mushrooms II: Prepare and sauté the mushroom caps as you would for stuffed mushrooms I, reserving the stems for another use. Cook chopped spinach according to package directions, or use fresh spinach, cooked and chopped. Drain the spinach well, pressing out all the liquid. Place the spinach in a saucepan over low heat to dry out the remaining liquid. Add enough heavy cream to moisten it, and cook it over low heat until the cream thickens slightly. Season it to taste with salt, white pepper, nutmeg, and onion powder. Pile the spinach high in the mushroom caps, and top each with a 1-inch homemade buttered crouton (see Index).

Stuffed mushrooms III: Prepare and sauté the caps as you would for stuffed mushrooms I, and remove the caps from the pan. Chop the stems fine and sauté them, sprinkling on ¼ teaspoon of lemon juice for each mushroom. In a small bowl, place one (4¾-ounce) can of liver spread for each six mushrooms. Add the mushroom stems and 1 tablespoon of light cream. Divide the mixture among the mushroom caps. Garnish the top of each with a shape cut from pimiento.

Stuffed tomatoes: Cut off the stem ends of medium-size, firm tomatoes; do not peel them. Using a sharp knife and a spoon, hollow out the tomatoes, removing and reserving about half of the pulp. Set the tomatoes upside down on paper towels. For each tomato, sauté 2 tablespoons of bread crumbs in butter until crisp. Add the tomato pulp, plus 1 tablespoon of chopped mushrooms and ½ teaspoon of finely chopped onion for each tomato. Continue to cook the mixture until it is almost dry. Add 1 teaspoon of light cream for each tomato. Remove the skillet from the heat and season the mixture to taste with salt, pepper, and dried basil or chopped fresh basil. Place the tomatoes in a baking dish. Divide the filling among them. Bake them in a 375°F. oven until they are hot, for 10 to 15 minutes. Using a small canapé cutter, cut shapes from sharp cheddar cheese. Place one shape on each tomato and return the tomatoes to the oven for 1 to 2 minutes, until the cheese has softened but has not lost its shape.

Stuffed onions: Peel medium, uniform-size onions and cook them in boiling salted water until they are almost tender. Remove them from the water and allow them to cool. Cut a slice off the stem end and, with a spoon, carefully scoop out the insides, leaving a ¼-inch-thick shell. Combine the onion pulp with bread crumbs, grated sharp cheese, and chopped ripe olives. Season the stuffing to taste with salt and pepper. Fill the onions with the mixture. Sprinkle the tops with buttered bread crumbs and additional grated cheese. Bake them in a 350°F. oven for 20 minutes, or until the onions are hot and the tops are nicely browned. Another time, omit the cheese; add chopped apple and season the filling with curry.

Stuffed zucchini: Cook whole zucchini briefly in boiling salted water until tender-crisp. When the zucchini are slightly cool, cut them in half lengthwise and, with a spoon, scoop a little pulp out of each half. Combine the pulp with coarsely crushed saltines. In butter, sauté finely chopped celery and minced garlic just until limp. Add a chopped raw or drained canned tomato, and cook the vegetables until most of the moisture is evaporated. Combine the celery and tomato with the pulp mixture, season it to taste with salt and pepper, and pile the mixture high into the zucchini shells. Bake in a 350°F. oven until the zucchini is hot; sprinkle them with paprika, and return them to the oven for 3 minutes.

Stuffed eggplant: Choose uniform-size small eggplants, no more than 4 inches long. Bake them whole in a 375°F. oven until they are barely soft. Cut them in half lengthwise and scoop out the pulp. Combine the pulp with finely minced onion, finely chopped tomato, chopped mushrooms, whole pine nuts (pignola), and minced parsley. Season the mixture to taste with garlic powder, salt, pepper, and oregano. Fill the shells with the stuffing, and then drizzle each half with ½ teaspoon of olive oil. Bake the eggplants in a 350°F. oven until they are hot. Cover them thickly with grated mozzarella cheese and sprinkle them with paprika. Return them to the oven for 3 to 4 minutes, until the cheese has softened but has not completely melted.

A garden of delights

"Flowers" made from whole vegetables look like a lot of trouble, but they really are not. They can be made in advance and are more than worth the few minutes spent on them.

Onion chrysanthemum: Peel a large onion and cut a thin slice off each end. Using a sharp knife, cut from close to the center through the outside edge and down to within ¼ inch of the bottom. Make 16 of these cuts, working evenly around the onion. Chill the onion in ice water. Drain it well; brush it lightly with vegetable oil, and sprinkle it with paprika. Or tint the ice water in which you chill the flower any color you like (but please, not blue!)—the onion will take on a lighter tint of the color. If you tint them, omit the paprika.

Beet roses I: Parboil large beets for 10 minutes, or until the skins will slip off. Remove them from the water and allow them to cool. Using a sharp knife, cut petal-shaped scallops around the lower edge of the beet, cutting close to, but not through, the bottom. Above these petals, cut off a ¼-inch-thick strip all the way around the beet. Starting ¼ inch above the row of petals, and between each two of the original petals, cut another row of scallops. Trim off another ¼-inch-thick strip as before. Repeat the cutting and trimming until you have reached the top of the beet, making four or five rows of petals.

Beet roses II: Peel large, raw beets. Using a vegetable peeler, pare long strips by working around the beet—try to get strips 6 to 8 inches long. Roll up these strips—fairly tightly to begin the rose, then more loosely as you progress—shaping them into full-blown roses. Secure the rose with a food pick if necessary.

Beet asters: Parboil and skin beets as you would to make beet roses I. Slice off the top quarter of the beet. Using a sharp knife, make parallel vertical cuts through the top of the beet to ¼ inch of the bottom. Make a second series of vertical cuts at right angles to the first. Chill the beets in ice water. Gently spread the petals of the flower before using.

Turnip asters: Using white turnips, follow the directions for making beet asters, above. Color the ice water in which you chill them if you wish.

Turnip roses: Pour boiling water over white turnips; let the turnips stand for 5 minutes, and then peel them. Follow the directions for beet roses I. To color these roses, dip them in water tinted with vegetable coloring and then drain them.

Tomato roses: Cut the peel from a large, firm tomato in one long strip, keeping the strip about 1 inch wide. Coil the peel tightly, making the bottom of the strip a bit tighter than the top. Secure the coil with a food pick if necessary. Use two sprigs of watercress as greenery for the rose.

Turnip lilies: For each lily—these are the calla lily type—cut two thin crosswise slices from a peeled raw turnip. Curve one slice into a cone shape. Curve the second slice around the first, in the opposite direction. For the pistil, insert a long, thin strip of carrot in the center of the cone. Secure the flower with a food pick, and chill it in ice water until it's crisp.

Any of these flowers, or an assortment of them, looks very handsome indeed as a garnish for a platter of meat, game, or poultry.

Curry favor with a crowd

Curry is another of those love-it-or-hate-it flavors. Those who love it speak of it in reverent tones, press on you their private recipe for curry seasoning or, if they are real fanatics, refuse to share the secret of their successful curry dishes.

A curry meal is a wonderful way to entertain. The main dish can be made ahead of time, for it improves with standing. And the delightful garnishes, called sambals, that dress the meal with their appearance and their contrasting flavors, can all be prepared in advance. Each sambal should be offered in a separate dish. Choose at least six or seven from this list:

chopped peanuts
toasted coconut
chopped (fresh or canned) mango
sliced radishes
thinly sliced scallions
chutney (recipes follow)
mustard pickles (from a jar)
sieved hard-cooked egg yolk

slivered garlic (for the hardy)
green pepper julienne
dried hot red pepper
india relish (from a jar)
pickled lemons or limes (from a jar)
chopped fresh coriander
thinly sliced bananas, sprinkled
  with chili powder

chopped hard-cooked egg white
grated raw turnip
pickled green chilies
crushed corn chips
tiny whole shrimp
lentils (cooked) in oil and vinegar
onion rings fried in olive oil
white raisins

chopped unpeeled apple
pomegranate seeds
chopped tomato
slivered preserved ginger
grated fresh ginger
dried peas (cooked) with lemon
    juice and paprika

Bombay duck, which is not duck at all but dried, salted fish, is another traditional garnish. Buy it in a gourmet food shop. Bake it in a hot oven until it is crisp and brown—the smell during preparation is rather off-putting, but the taste is great.

You can buy bottled chutney, of course. But you can also make your own, and the result will be delightful in both taste and appearance. Try one of these unusual varieties.

APRICOT CHUTNEY
about 4 cups

2 cups dried apricots, quartered
2 tablespoons sliced candied
    ginger
1 cup white raisins
1 cup chopped onions
1½ cups firmly packed dark
    brown sugar
½ lemon, thinly sliced and
    quartered

½ cup wine vinegar
2 cloves garlic, crushed
1½ teaspoons dry mustard
1 teaspoon crushed hot red pepper
½ cup tomato juice
½ teaspoon salt
½ teaspoon cinnamon
½ teaspoon ground cloves
½ teaspoon allspice

Combine all ingredients in a heavy saucepan. Simmer over low heat until thick, about 30 minutes. Cover and refrigerate.

CRANBERRY CHUTNEY
about 7 cups

1 (1-pound) package fresh
    cranberries
2 cups sugar
1 cup orange juice
1 cup white raisins

1 cup chopped walnuts
1 cup chopped celery
1 medium apple, cored and chopped
1 tablespoon grated orange peel
1 teaspoon ground ginger

Place cranberries and sugar in a heavy saucepan. Add 1 cup water; bring to a boil, stirring frequently. Reduce heat and simmer 15 minutes. Remove from heat, stir in remaining ingredients. Cover and refrigerate.

Base your curry on lamb, chicken, or beef—whatever meat you prefer. Add one of the Indian breads—chapattis, parathas, nan roti, puris, poppadums—bought at a specialty food shop or made at home from recipes in a good international cookbook. Cook the rice, without which no

Opposite: Ham en croute and lemon cups

40

curry meal is complete, with a little butter or oil in the water so that every grain will stand up and glisten; season the rice with a little saffron or turmeric to give it a golden glow, and encircle it with flat-leaf parsley (cilantro) for contrast. As a salad, offer sliced cucumbers dressed with yogurt and mint. Plan on beer to drink—wine and curry are not good friends—and have another cool beverage, such as iced tea or coffee or tall glasses of coconut milk, for those who don't want beer. Fruit is ideal for dessert, or crisp crackers with cream cheese and guava jelly. The whole meal is beautiful to look at, delightful to eat—and makes a great party.

Ham, in all its glory

Ham is an old standby for entertaining, and so it should be, for almost everyone likes it. And there's almost always a bonus of ham leftovers to provide the family with one or two substantial meals, sometimes a bone to flavor a pea or lentil soup, as well as some savory scraps to scramble with eggs for Sunday brunch. So, besides being good, ham is a good investment. And it can be very impressive to look at as well.

A ham of any kind—whole or half, bone-in or boneless, mild-cured or with hearty salt-smoke country flavor—profits in both looks and flavor from being glazed. Prepare the ham according to the directions on the wrapper or the can; before serving, bake the ham on a rack in a 350°F. oven until the internal temperature reaches 130°F.—this is all the cooking a fully cooked ham will need—crisscross the top and sides with cuts about ½ inch deep, and dress it with one of the following glazes. Use the glaze alone, or decorate it as indicated. Increase the oven temperature to 400°F. Return the ham to the oven until the glaze is set and hot, for 15 to 20 minutes.

British pub-style glaze: Combine ½ cup of firmly packed dark brown sugar, ¼ cup of dark beer, ½ teaspoon of summer savory, and ¼ teaspoon of basil. Spoon the glaze over the ham and return it to the oven. Garnish the ham with thick sautéed tomato slices and serve it with brussels sprouts or panned cabbage.

New England-style glaze: Stud the ham with whole cloves where the cuts intersect. Pat maple sugar thickly over the ham, or spoon maple syrup on it. Garnish the ham with sautéed pineapple rings before serving.

Midwest-style glaze: Combine 1 cup of orange marmalade, ¼ cup of cider vinegar, and ¼ teaspoon of nutmeg. Spread the glaze over the ham and return the ham to the oven. Cut ¼-inch slices from navel oranges. Cut canned cranberry jelly into ¼-inch slices and then, with a small cookie or canapé cutter, cut a star shape from each slice of jelly. Center a cranberry star on each orange slice and use these to garnish the platter on which the ham is served.

Deep South-style glaze: Spoon honey over a Smithfield or other country-style ham and return the ham to the oven until it is lightly browned. Garnish the serving platter with spiced crabapples or sautéed apple slices.

Island-style glaze: Sprinkle the ham thickly with light brown sugar and decorate it with half slices of pineapple and pieces of candied ginger (hold them in place with food picks). Return the ham to the oven. Garnish the serving platter with pieces of sautéed bananas alternating with mounds of mashed yams seasoned with cinnamon.

California-style glaze: Combine 1 thawed can of undiluted frozen orange juice concentrate, 1 cup of brown sugar, and ¼ cup of A1 Sauce. Spoon the glaze over the ham and return the ham to the oven. Garnish the serving platter with orange segments and mint sprigs.

Madeira-style glaze: Pour 1 cup of Madeira wine over the ham before baking it. To glaze the ham, sprinkle it lightly with brown sugar, spoon over it 1 additional cup of wine, and return it to the oven. Garnish the serving platter with bunches of red and purple grapes and grape leaves. Serve the ham with a sauce made of 1 cup of beef broth and 1 cup of Madeira, cooked and thickened slightly with cornstarch.

Georgia-style glaze: Combine 1 cup of peach nectar and ½ cup of honey. Spoon the glaze over the ham and return the ham to the oven. Garnish the serving platter with brandied peaches (see Index).

Sometimes a ham—particularly a canned or boneless one, which may have great flavor but not look all that much like a ham—profits from wearing a coat of pastry. You can use your favorite pie crust recipe, or frozen patty-shell pastry (see Index), or try this: Bake a 5-pound fully cooked ham in a preheated 325°F. oven until its internal temperature reaches 140°F. Remove it from the oven and cool it for 20 minutes. Spread ½ cup of pineapple preserves over the ham and sprinkle it lightly with nutmeg. Separate the dough from 1 (8-ounce) can of refrigerated crescent dinner rolls into two large rectangles; press the perforations together to seal the dough. Overlap the long sides of the rectangles and roll the dough out to form one 13- x 9-inch rectangle. Place the dough over the ham, covering the top and sides. Trim the excess dough from the corners; cut the excess into small oval shapes, like flower petals, and position them in groups of three on the crust. Increase the oven temperature to 375°F. Bake the ham for 13 to 15 minutes, until the crust is lightly browned. Remove the ham from the oven and brush the crust with melted butter. Halve candied cherries and use them as centers for the pastry "flowers." This ham will yield eight to ten servings. Garnish the serving platter with lemon cups (see Index) filled alternately with currant jelly and with sour cream into which prepared mustard and horseradish to taste has been stirred. Tuck bits of parsley or watercress between the lemon cups for added color.

Homemade jewels

Sweet-tart jellies flavored with herbs and spices make wonderfully pretty and delicious garnishes. Put up in small decorative glasses or molds, they can be turned out to enhance a hot or cold main dish. Almost any meat, poultry, or game takes kindly to these jewel-tone accompaniments.

In all cases, have the jelly glasses, molds, or whatever containers you're going to use, and their lids, sterilized and ready, and have melted paraffin on hand. If you are going to use containers that do not have lids, paraffin the top of the jelly, allow it to cool, then cover the container with foil or paper tied in place to protect the paraffin.

SPICED TOMATO JELLY
six 1-cup containers

3¼ pounds ripe tomatoes, stemmed and quartered
1 whole nutmeg, lightly crushed
2 (3-inch) sticks cinnamon, broken
1½ teaspoons whole cloves
½ teaspoon ground allspice

¾ teaspoon red food coloring (optional)
¼ cup cider vinegar
1 (1¾-ounce) package powdered pectin
4½ cups sugar

In a heavy 5-quart pan, combine tomatoes, nutmeg, cinnamon, cloves, allspice, food coloring, vinegar, and 1 cup water. Bring to a boil. Reduce heat, cover, and simmer, stirring occasionally, 45 minutes. Press through a wire strainer. Discard spices and tomato skins. Return tomato juice to pan; bring to a boil. Pour the hot juice into a wire strainer lined with a clean muslin cloth wrung out in cold water. Allow to drip, stirring occasionally, until the residue in the strainer is dry. Measure tomato juice; you should have 3 cups—if not, add water or boil juice down to get this amount. Combine the 3 cups juice with pectin in a 5-quart pan; bring to a boil, stirring occasionally. Add sugar all at once; bring to a full boil that cannot be stirred down. Boil hard 1 minute, stirring constantly. Remove from heat, let stand 1 minute. Carefully skim off foam. Pour into prepared containers to ⅛ inch from top. Cover with melted paraffin or use jar lids, following manufacturer's directions.

HERB JELLIES
each jelly: four 1-cup containers

for all jellies use:
    3¼ cups sugar, divided

½ bottle liquid pectin

for Basil Jelly use also:
    2 tablespoons basil
    1 cup tomato juice

¼ cup lemon juice
¼ cup water

for Lemon Thyme Jelly use also:
    1½ tablespoons lemon thyme
    1 cup dry red wine

½ cup water

for Sweet Marjoram Jelly use also:

2 tablespoons sweet marjoram	¼ cup lime juice
1 cup pineapple juice	¼ cup water

for Sage Jelly use also:

1 tablespoon sage	¼ cup water
1¼ cups dry red wine	

for Rosemary Jelly use also:

1½ tablespoons rosemary	¼ cup lime juice
¼ cup orange juice	¾ cup water

To make any one of these jellies: Wash the leaves of the fresh herb, spread out to dry; cut into small pieces; measure pieces. Crush herb with ¼ cup of the sugar. Place in a heavy 4-quart pan. Stir in the required liquids. Bring to a boil; simmer 8 minutes. Bring to a rolling boil, stir in pectin; boil ½ minute, stirring constantly. Add remaining 3 cups sugar all at once; bring to a full boil that cannot be stirred down; boil 1 minute. Remove from heat, let stand 1 minute. Skim off foam. Pour through a fine sieve into prepared containers. Cover with paraffin or jar lids.

Little dumplings, light as air

A garland of tiny dumplings, with sprigs of parsley or watercress tucked in among them, makes a delicious main-dish garnish and adds substance to the dish as well. Experiment with these delectable mouthfuls.

Gnocchi: Into a 4-egg recipe for pâte à chou (cream-puff pastry) stir ¾ cup grated parmesan cheese and ⅛ teaspoon of cayenne pepper. Drop a few scant teaspoonfuls at a time into simmering salted water; cook until the dumplings rise to the top. Place the cooked gnocchi in the oven to keep them warm. To serve, sprinkle the gnocchi with additional parmesan, then with paprika. Gnocchi are delicious with ham, with lamb, and—surprisingly—with fried chicken.

Mousselines: Cut the meat of a ½-pound breast of chicken into small pieces. (Lean veal may be used if you prefer.) Season the pieces with ¼ teaspoon of salt and a dash of white pepper. Pound the meat in a mortar or put it through the finest blade of a food chopper, gradually adding 1 egg white. Rub the ground mixture through a fine sieve into a pan. Place the pan on a bed of ice and work the mixture with a wooden spoon until it is chilled. Gradually add 1 cup of heavy cream, working it in a little at a time. (This mixture is called forcemeat.) Butter a deep skillet. Pile the forcemeat into a tablespoon; press another tablespoon over it to form a small egg shape. Slide the forcemeat gently off the spoon into the skillet. When all the mousselines are formed, add a little salted water or chicken stock to the skillet. Bring the liquid to a boil. Lower the heat and poach the mousselines gently for 10 to 15 minutes, until they are firm. Do not

45

let the liquid boil or the mousselines will break up. Remove the mousse-lines gently with a slotted spoon and place them on a towel to drain. Use them to garnish any delicately flavored poultry or veal dish. For a fish or shellfish dish, make the forcemeat of any firm, white-fleshed fish. French recipes calling for mousselines presuppose that you always have a few truffles in your kitchen and suggest that you decorate each mous-seline with a shape cut from a truffle. Lacking truffles—as most of us do most of the time—use shapes cut from ripe olives.

Kin to these dumplings—not as float-away light, but hearty and with excellent flavor—is our very American hasty pudding, sliced and fried. Served with ham or any other kind of pork, or with chicken, turkey, or game birds, it makes an unusual garnish.

Hasty pudding: Bring 2½ cups of water and ¾ teaspoon of salt to a boil in a deep, heavy kettle. Gradually add 1 cup of yellow cornmeal, stirring constantly. Reduce the heat and simmer the cornmeal for 30 minutes, stirring occasionally. Rinse a loaf pan with cold water; spoon the corn-meal mixture into it. Refrigerate the pudding several hours or overnight, until it is firm. Turn out the pudding and cut it into ¾-inch-thick slices. Heat fat in a heavy skillet and pan-fry the pudding slices until they are brown and crusty on both sides. To use as a garnish, top each fried slice with a bacon curl, a dab of currant jelly, or a shape cut from cranberry jelly. Fried hasty pudding can also be used as a base on which to spoon creamed chicken or ham, or it can be served with butter and syrup (and sausage, bacon, or fried ham) at breakfast or brunch.

Is there anyone who doesn't like chestnuts?

Almost any nuts are useful and delicious to use in garnishing, but chest-nuts have a special place in many people's hearts. Admittedly, they're a nuisance to prepare, but they can be cooked in advance—any good general cookbook will tell you how—or you can, fortunately, buy them in cans already shelled, skinned, and cooked.

Cooked whole chestnuts can be gently sautéed in butter to form a border garnish for turkey, game, beef, or lamb; or a border of chestnut purée can be piped (or mounded with a spoon) around the same foods.

Chestnut purée: In a saucepan, combine 2 drained (11-ounce) cans of whole chestnuts, 1 (10½-ounce) can of condensed consommé, and ½ cup of finely chopped celery. Simmer the mixture until the consommé is absorbed; then press it through a sieve or whirl it in a blender. Stir in 1 tablespoon of soft butter and ⅓ cup of light cream.

Some like it cold

Cold foods are wonderful for hot-weather entertaining; prepared in advance they wait patiently in your refrigerator until serving time—even if that moment is delayed, as so often happens—while you enjoy your own party. A mousse of chicken or of salmon or other fish, or shrimps in a mold of lemon-spiked madrilène, or a hearty salad or old-fashioned pressed chicken—any of these makes a most inviting main dish for a hot-weather party. So does a cold glazed ham, or cold chicken breasts, or a bountiful platter of various kinds of cold meats. Brought to the table beautifully garnished, any of these will be fallen on with shouts of joy by ravenous guests you thought would not be hungry on such a hot day.

If you are making a mousse or other food that will be turned out of its mold, garnish it by following the directions for garnishing uncooked pâtés. Pressed chicken or pressed veal profits by the same kind of treatment. Any of these looks far prettier, too, if served on a bed of greens. Nasturtium leaves and some of the flowers are particularly pretty with a pale-colored mold, such as a chicken mousse. Or serve a cold main dish on a bed of chopped aspic for a deliciously cool effect. In making aspic, use chicken stock for poultry dishes, beef for meat dishes, and fish stock (or bottled clam juice) for fish dishes. Make the stock from a recipe in any standard cookbook, or used canned beef or chicken bouillon or consommé; if you use the canned condensed kind, dilute it with only ½ cup of water.

For sparkling aspic, cloudless as a summer sky, you must clarify the stock.

Clarified stock: Place 2 quarts of cold, fat-free stock in a large saucepan. Beat 3 egg whites lightly and stir them into the stock. Add the egg shells —an essential part of the secret of clear stock. Heat the stock slowly to boiling, stirring constantly with a slotted spoon. (This will take a while and is admittedly boring. Stir with one hand and hold a book with the other—you might as well enjoy yourself.) When the mixture reaches a full boil, there will be a layer of sticky sediment on top. Set the pan aside, undisturbed, for 15 minutes. Then pour the stock through a strainer lined with several thicknesses of cheesecloth wrung out in cold water. Let it drain for 15 minutes. Use the stock at once or refrigerate it, uncovered.

Perfect aspic: Pour 1 quart of cold, clarified stock into a saucepan; over it sprinkle 2 tablespoons (envelopes) of unflavored gelatin. Place the mixture over low heat and stir it until the stock is clear and the gelatin is dissolved. Cool the aspic and use as directed in recipes, or pour it into a pan, about ¾-inch deep, and refrigerate it until it is firmly set. When it is set, chop it coarsely with a heavy knife. Use chopped aspic to surround any cold, molded food. For example, put it around a fish aspic that has been molded in a fish-shaped form, with bits of unpeeled cucumber set in aspic for scales and tail and a slice of stuffed olive for an eye. To garnish the platter, cut slices of lemon and slit them from the center to the peel; pull the two loose pieces gently in opposite directions and thread a bit of dill through the resulting twist. Instead of chopping the aspic, it can be cut into shapes with cookie or canapé cutters to place on greens around any chilled food.

Here are two wonderful ham-and-aspic combinations to grace any hot-weather buffet table or serve as the main dish for a sit-down meal. **Jambon persillé:** In a heavy saucepan, combine 3½ cups of well-flavored chicken stock, 2 tablespoons of lemon juice, 6 black peppercorns, 1 bay leaf, 2 tablespoons of minced onion, ¼ teaspoon of dried thyme, 1 teaspoon of dried tarragon, and 2 whole cloves. Bring the mixture to a boil. Reduce the heat; cover and simmer the mixture for 10 minutes. Strain the mixture, return it to the pan, and add 2 tablespoons (envelopes) of unflavored gelatin. Clarify it (described above) with 2 egg whites and 2 egg shells. Measure the stock and add enough dry white wine to make 3½ cups of liquid. Allow it to cool. In a 2-quart mold, place 5 cups of cubed ham and 1 cup of finely chopped parsley; mix them well. Pour the cooled gelatin liquid into the mold. Cover the gelatin and refrigerate it overnight, or until it is set. Decorate the platter with chopped perfect aspic (see above) and lemon cups (see Index) filled with mayonnaise seasoned to taste with lemon juice, garlic juice, and dijon mustard. Top the mayonnaise in each lemon cup with three capers. Or omit the garlic juice and capers and stir chopped mixed candied fruit into the mustard mayonnaise. **Easy lemon-aspic ham:** Chill a 5-pound ready-to-eat ham. Dissolve 1 (3-ounce) package of lemon-flavored gelatin in 1 cup of boiling water; add ½ cup of cold water. Refrigerate the gelatin until it reaches the consistency of thick syrup, for about 10 minutes. Place the ham on a rack over a tray; spoon the gelatin over its top and sides to form a thin layer. Refrigerate the ham, but do not refrigerate the remaining gelatin. When the glaze on the ham is set, after about 15 minutes, spoon on another layer of the unrefrigerated gelatin. Cut thin, crosswise slices of raw carrot, beet, or turnip, and cut the slices into petal shapes with a canapé cutter or a sharp knife. Dip the petal shapes into the gelatin and place them on the ham. Cut pieces of cucumber peel for stems and leaves; dip them into the gelatin and set them in place. Refrigerate the ham for 15 minutes; spoon another thin layer of glaze over all. (If necessary, the gelatin that has collected in the tray may be strained, heated, and cooled to the proper consistency to be used for this last layer.) Refrigerate the ham until serving time. You may use this same quick and easy method to glaze a boneless turkey roll or a piece of poached fresh salmon or any other fish.

To make a handsome cold platter, mask cold poached fish, chicken breasts, or sliced chicken or turkey with mayonnaise collée, also called mayonnaise chaud-froid. This, unlike the aspics, is not transparent. Here is a particularly delicious way to prepare this old standby of French cooking. Depending on what food you are going to mask, you may leave the mayonnaise as it is in the recipe or flavor it lightly with curry powder, dry mustard, or grated orange or lemon peel.

Mayonnaise collée: Sprinkle 1 tablespoon (envelope) of unflavored gelatin over ¼ cup of cold chicken broth (water will do if you don't have broth); dissolve the gelatin by stirring it over hot water in a small double boiler. Cool the gelatin slightly and stir it into 1 cup of mayonnaise; stir in 2 tablespoons of lemon juice and refrigerate the mixture for 15 minutes. Fold in ½ cup of heavy cream, which has been whipped.

Here is a variation of another traditional mask—chaud-froid sauce.

Chaud-froid glaze: In a saucepan, sprinkle 2 tablespoons (envelopes) of unflavored gelatin over 2½ cups of cold, fat-free chicken broth and stir the mixture over low heat until the gelatin dissolves. Stir 1 teaspoon of dry mustard into 3 tablespoons of Madeira wine or cream sherry. Add this mixture to the broth and cool it slightly. Then gradually stir in 1 cup of dairy sour cream and 1 cup of heavy cream and season the mixture with ⅛ teaspoon of salt. Refrigerate the mixture until it is thick but not set, stirring often. Use the glaze for any of the meats above, or for a whole boneless ham or sliced ham.

To use either the delicate mayonnaise collée or the slightly more robust chaud-froid glaze, spoon part of the mixture in a thin, even layer over the food to be masked. Refrigerate the food a few minutes, until the glaze sets. Spoon on a second layer and, before the mixture sets, put in place whatever decoration you wish to use—fresh herbs, shapes cut from vegetables or from fruit peels, or a combination of both. Refrigerate the dish until serving time. As you work with chaud-froid glaze, you may need to chill or warm the glaze briefly in order to keep it thick but spoonable. To do so, set its container in a pan of ice water or warm water.

Should you wish to experiment with the standard chaud-froid sauce, any good international cookbook will provide you with a recipe—or, probably, two recipes, one for the white version (Chaud-Froid Blanc) and one for the brown (Chaud-Froid Brun). Some elaborate French recipes call for masking food with one or the other of these sauces and then, as a final touch, gilding with aspic over the sauce. This is a lot of work, but the result is spectacular.

If you plan to serve a platter of sliced cold meats, you may cover them with thin layers of perfect aspic (see Index), or with either mayonnaise collée or chaud-froid glaze. Or you may, certainly, leave the meats (and/or fish, and/or poultry) unglazed and decorate the platter in various ways. One of the most interesting ways—and one that will add savor and substance to the meal—is to ring the platter with molded oeufs en gelée (eggs in aspic).

Eggs in aspic: Combine 2 cups of clear chicken broth, 1 teaspoon of dried tarragon leaves, and 1 chopped shallot or green onion and simmer the mixture for 10 minutes. Cover and cool the broth. Strain and measure it; add more broth if necessary to make 2 cups. Return the broth to the saucepan; sprinkle on 1 tablespoon (envelope) of unflavored gelatin, and stir the broth over low heat until the gelatin is dissolved. Spoon a layer of the aspic mixture into each of four small molds; refrigerate them until the aspic is firm. Refrigerate the remainder of the aspic until it has the consistency of thick syrup. Dip watercress leaves into the aspic and place three on the set aspic in each mold. Refrigerate the molds a few moments; place a chilled poached egg (or egg mollet) into each cup and spoon the remaining aspic over them. Refrigerate them until the aspic is set, for about 2 hours.

Eggs may also be molded in canned consommé madrilène. With the addition of julienne strips of ham or tongue, these eggs—in aspic or madrilène—make a delightful luncheon dish. Unmold them on lettuce leaves, garnish them with a lemon wedge and more watercress, and serve them with mustard-flavored mayonnaise.

Whether or not you add eggs in aspic to your cold meat platter, be sure that there is greenery of some kind—watercress, parsley, grape or nasturtium or celery leaves, endive, escarole, butter or bibb lettuce—decorating the platter. Use any of the flower vegetable shapes—roses, chrysanthemums, lilies, or such (see Index)—to make a handsome and inviting platter.

A savory salad—potato or macaroni, one of the slaws, or well-dressed greens—in tomato cups makes a fine accompaniment to cold meats. Choose medium-size, firm, unpeeled tomatoes; halve them crosswise and scoop out the centers, leaving ¼-inch-thick walls. Leave the edges as they are or, if you like, make a sawtooth pattern, using a sharp knife to cut the edge of each cup into points. Fill the cups with salad. Halved, scooped-out sweet red or green peppers also make handsome containers for such salads.

When fresh cherries are in season, halve and pit them, saving the stems. Put two halves back together with blue cheese—mixed with milk or cream to spreading consistency—between them. Replace the stems and pile these delicious mouthfuls on your cold meat platter.

To make celery rosettes, cut off the top and base of one bunch of celery; wash the stalks and pat them dry with paper towels. Beat 1 (8-ounce) package of softened cream cheese with 1 tablespoon of milk, 1 tablespoon of snipped chives, ½ teaspoon of curry powder, and ⅛ teaspoon of salt, until they are well blended. Fill the celery stalks with the mixture. Regroup the stalks into the shape of the original bunch, starting with the smallest stalks in the center, pressing each firmly into place as you go. Wrap the stalks tightly in foil and refrigerate them for 2 to 3 hours. Just before serving, cut the bunch into crosswise slices and use the slices to garnish a platter of cold meats.

Packaged cold cuts can be shaped to garnish a cheese—cold cuts platter. Curve thin slices of bologna, summer sausage, salami, or other round sliced meats into cornucopias; hold them in place with food picks. Fill them with a savory cheese mixture or a dab of salad, or simply tuck in a sprig of parsley or watercress. To make a bologna pinwheel, use a sharp knife to cut each round slice into quarters to within ½ inch of the center; fold every other corner in toward the center and fasten it with a piece of a food pick. Top the center with half a stuffed olive. Three of these at either end of a platter, each set on a lettuce leaf, make an attractive garnish.

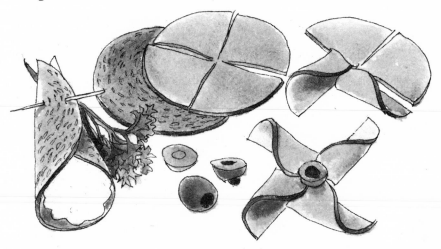

Smaller shapes made from vegetables—radish roses, carrot curlicues, cherry-tomato rosettes, and such (see Index: vegetable shapes) can also be used to dress up platters of cold meat, fish, or poultry.

Whatever you choose to serve as a main dish, hot or cold, there is an attractive and suitable garnish for it. However you garnish your main dishes, they will be better looking and better tasting because you've taken the little extra time and effort required. And the bonus is this: You'll enjoy doing it. You'll get into the spirit of garnishing once you've tried some of the decorations you've read about here, and then let your imagination guide you into inventing new garnishes for every dish you serve to your family or to guests.

Garnishing Sandwiches

A sandwich crouching alone on a plate (particularly a too-large plate) is a pretty forlorn object, no matter how rewarding its flavor may be. But a garnished sandwich, on a pretty plate that just nicely accommodates it and its accompaniments, is a pleasure to the eye, a temptation to the appetite. Almost anything will cheer up its looks and taste—a couple of olives, a brace of pickle slices, a handful of potato chips. But you can do better.

Any of the smaller vegetable shapes (see Index) will add to a sand-

wich's appeal. Or try a slice or two of celery rosette or a few blue-cheese cherries (see Index). Or stuff small stalks of celery with sharp cheddar cheese moistened with cream or mayonnaise and sprinkle them with chopped walnuts. Or stuff blades of belgian endive with softened cream cheese, and sprinkle them liberally with snipped chives. Impale a slippery sandwich with a food pick; stick something tasty on the top of it—an olive, a pickle, a pickled onion, a fat grape, a preserved kumquat, a mandarin orange section, a cube of cheese. If you're serving a help-yourself platter of sandwiches, garnish the plate with one or the other of the following two tomato creations, making enough so that each guest can have one.

Tomato–cheese roses: Dip small, firm tomatoes into boiling water for 3 or 4 seconds; slip off the skins. Refrigerate the tomatoes for at least 30 minutes. Meanwhile, beat lightly salted, softened cream cheese until it is fluffy. To form the petals of the rose, fill a small, pointed teaspoon with the cream cheese, then level the cheese off with the back of a knife. Hold the tomato rounded-side up. Press the cheese-filled teaspoon against the side of the tomato near the top, sliding the cheese onto the tomato with a downward stroke of the spoon. Repeat, working around the tomato. Depending on the size of the tomato, make one or two more rows of petals beneath the first row. Refrigerate the tomatoes until serving time. Sprinkle the centers of the tomatoes with sieved hard-cooked egg yolk and place them on small lettuce leaves on the sandwich platter.
Cherry-tomato flowers: You'll need small cherry tomatoes and the same number of medium-size ones. Use the larger one first. Cut each in half from the blossom end almost to the stem end. Cut each of the resulting halves into four sections in the same manner, so that the tomato will open into eight petals, all connected at the bottom. Using a spoon, gently remove the seeds and most of the flesh from each petal. Cut the cherry tomatoes the same way, but cut each half into three sections; remove the seeds and flesh. Place a cherry tomato inside each larger tomato. Fasten each flower with a piece of a food pick at the center and put a small shape cut from a slice of carrot on the top of the pick. These can remain at room temperature, covered with damp paper towels, until you're ready to use them. Place them on greens on the sandwich platter.

Opposite: Salmon Mousse

53

The provident hen, bless her

A deviled egg is an excellent garnish for a sandwich plate. Vary the flavor of the yolk mixture to suit the sandwich filling. Children love deviled eggs —so do adults—and besides adding eye- and taste-appeal, they turn a simple sandwich into a meal of substance.

Basic deviled eggs: Shell and chill six hard-cooked eggs. Halve them lengthwise. Remove the yolks carefully; press them through a sieve or mash them with a fork. Add about 1 tablespoon of mayonnaise—enough to make a smooth, light paste. Season the paste to taste with salt and cayenne pepper. Lightly mound the yolk mixture in the whites. Refrigerate the eggs until serving time.

Butter-deviled eggs: Shell, but do not chill six hard-cooked eggs. Remove the yolks as above. Into the still-warm yolks, incorporate 1 to 2 tablespoons of whipped butter. Season the yolk mixture to taste and mound it in the whites.

Either of the above deviled eggs will be bland—right for the very young, rather nothing-tasting for their elders. Perk them up by adding to the yolk mixture any one, or a combination, of these:

1½ teaspoons worcestershire sauce	2 teaspoons snipped chives
1 teaspoon dry mustard	1 tablespoon chopped dill or
¼ cup grated sharp cheddar cheese	sweet pickle
1 tablespoon grated onion	¼ cup shredded raw spinach
2 drops garlic juice	1 tablespoon finely chopped radish
½ teaspoon anchovy paste	¼ teaspoon curry powder
2 tablespoons mashed liver sausage	4 skinless, boneless sardines
4 finely chopped whole raw	2 tablespoons deviled ham or
mushrooms	ground tongue

2 tablespoons crumbled cooked bacon	¼ cup tiny shrimp, halved
2 tablespoons shredded smoked salmon	2 tablespoons softened blue cheese
	½ teaspoon dried basil or oregano

Devil dress-ups: To complete the deviled eggs you use as garnishes for sandwiches, decorate the top of each filled half with one of these: a sprig of watercress or parsley; three or four drained capers; a piece of water chestnut rolled in chopped parsley or paprika; an asparagus tip seated in a dab of lemon-spiked mayonnaise; an anchovy fillet, halved and the halves crossed, or a rolled anchovy fillet; crossed thin strips of pimiento; a small wedge of cheese, buried point down; a small wedge of sweet red or green pepper, buried point down; a drift of paprika or chopped parsley.

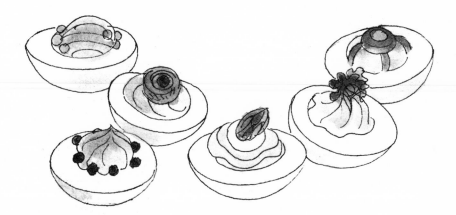

Some homemade sit-besides

Vegetable garnishes in one form or another seem to be perfect partners for meat, fish, or poultry sandwiches—they're pleasant to see on the sandwich plate and a delicious contrast to the sandwich itself.

Artichoke hearts vinaigrette: Cook 1 package of frozen artichoke hearts according to package directions and drain. Combine ¼ cup of wine vinegar, ¼ cup of olive oil, 1 teaspoon of salt, ¼ teaspoon of freshly ground pepper. Marinate the artichoke hearts in the mixture for at least 4 hours.

Asparagus vinaigrette: Marinate cooked fresh or frozen asparagus as above; if you like, substitute cider vinegar and vegetable oil for the wine vinegar and olive oil.

Mushrooms à la grecque: Marinate raw or briefly cooked sliced fresh mushrooms in ¼ cup of lemon juice, ¼ cup of olive oil, and ½ teaspoon of salt. If you like, add a little onion juice to the marinade.

Spring garden mélange: In a bowl, combine chopped celery, diced cucumber, thinly sliced radishes, chopped green pepper, sliced scallions (include some of the green tops), and chopped parsley in whatever proportions suit you. Add just enough dairy sour cream to hold the mixture together. Season the vegetables liberally with salt and freshly ground pepper. (If you prefer, or if waistlines dictate, add cottage cheese whirled in the blender instead of sour cream.) Serve the vegetables in a lettuce cup— a refreshing complement to almost any sandwich.

Salad on the side

Virtually any sort of salad that comes to your mind will go well and look well with a sandwich. A portion of potato or macaroni salad on a lettuce leaf or in a tomato cup (see Index) or a green pepper cup (see Index) makes a light sandwich hearty and gives the sandwich plate the appearance of really offering something to eat. Or, for good looks and good eating, try one of these.

Somebody's salad: The British call it French Salad, the French call it Russian Salad, and goodness knows what the Russians call it, but it's delicious—and a great way to use up leftover vegetables. Any combination is good—peas, cubed carrots or potatoes, lima beans, green or wax beans, corn, cauliflower, whatever. Combine ½ cup each of any three cold cooked vegetables, ½ cup of diced celery, 2 tablespoons of minced onion, and 1 tablespoon of drained capers. Season the vegetables lightly with salt and bind them with just enough mayonnaise to hold them together. If you like, omit the capers and substitute ¼ teaspoon of garlic powder. A version of this, using just tiny cooked peas and carrot cubes bound with mayonnaise, is called Italian Salad by the Scandinavians.

Dilled cucumbers: Slice cucumbers (peeled or not, as you choose) very thin and sprinkle them with salt. Weight them with a heavy china plate and let them stand for 2 hours. Rinse the slices in cold water, drain them, and place them in a bowl. For every two cucumbers, combine ½ cup of vinegar, 2 tablespoons each of water and sugar, ⅛ teaspoon of white pepper, and 1 tablespoon of chopped fresh dill. Pour the mixture over the cucumbers and toss them. Refrigerate the cucumbers at least 1 hour before serving.

Fruit for some

A light, mild-flavored sandwich—chicken, say, or cream cheese on orange or date-nut bread—calls for a fruit garnish. Try spears of fresh pineapple rolled in chopped mint, or slices of orange lightly sprinkled with brown sugar and dressed with a dab of dairy sour cream. Or offer a spiced or pickled fruit (see Index). If you're serving a fish sandwich, accompany it with tartar sauce in a lemon cup (see Index).

Cool green-yellow slices of avocado, sprinkled with lemon juice, are handsome and delicious. Sprinkle grapefruit sections very lightly with curry powder, or sprinkle them a bit more heavily with turmeric. Fill half a peeled, pitted fresh peach with shredded cheddar cheese mixed with chopped pecans, or a pear with a ball of cream cheese rolled in chopped parsley. If you're feeling ambitious, french fry slices of slightly under-ripe banana, just as you'd french fry potatoes, for a pretty, what-is-it? sandwich garnish.

Cheese- or nut-stuffed prunes go well with sandwiches. So do chunks of mango or papaya, or thin wedges of peeled cantaloupe or honeydew melon, or an incredibly beautiful peeled, halved chinese gooseberry (kiwi fruit). Dress any of these with a squeeze of lime juice and a sprinkling of salt.

Nuts for others

Think of any sandwich with which you enjoy a potato-chip garnish. You'll like it even better garnished with nuts. Any of the commercial salted nuts works well. Smokehouse almonds go well with a ham or corned-beef sandwich; macadamia nuts seem just right with a chicken-salad sandwich.

You'll be surprised and delighted at the results if you try your hand at roasting and seasoning nuts at home.

Fresh-roasted nuts: Spread 2 pounds of any kind of raw shelled nut on a jelly roll pan. Or use several kinds in combination. Drizzle the nuts with ⅓ cup of sesame or vegetable oil. Bake them at 350°F. until they are delicately browned, for about 15 minutes. Watch them closely, or they'll be too well toasted. Season the nuts by sprinkling with salt, or with salt and chili powder or curry powder. Or omit the salt and sprinkle them with superfine granulated sugar, then with cinnamon or mace or ginger.

The bigger, better burger

For youngsters and grownups alike, hamburgers cooked in the back yard can be a big treat. Next time you entertain at a burger party, bear this in mind: a hamburger is good, a vastburger is fabulous. And a vast-burger looks great, too, which is more than you can say for your average hamburger.

What's a vastburger? It could also be called a hugeburger, or per-haps a mammothburger. In other words, a big, giant, overgrown, whop-ping hamburger. The day before serving, make up a package of hot roll mix—or two, if you're thinking big. Shape the dough, before baking, into a big hamburger bun shape (or two). Bake the bun at the temperature specified by the package directions for about 18 minutes, until it is a rich golden brown. When you remove it from the oven, brush the top with soft butter for a pretty, golden crust. Cool the bun, and wrap it in foil until the next day, when you will shape the seasoned beef into a big, fit-the-bun hamburger patty. (Mix six parts beef to one part chipped ice—that's right, ice—for the tenderest, juiciest hamburger ever created. No fooling.) Cook the patty on the grill to the desired degree of doneness—rare, hopefully—topping it, when you turn the patty over, with softened blue cheese or a big drift of shredded swiss and a sprinkle of chili powder. Place the patty on the bottom of the bun, sprinkle it with sliced scallions, put the top of the bun in place, and cut the burger in wedges to serve. Offer cuts of fresh dill pickle, crisp slices of bread-and-butter pickle, and a pot of catsup—with mustard and horseradish added—which has been heated on the grill—and stand back to listen to the deafening applause.

Those dandy Danes

Danish smørrebrød—the open-face sandwiches that are sheer poetry for both eye and palate—is Denmark's national dish. A smørrebrød luncheon or supper can be a wonderful, unusual way to entertain. Set platters of these savory sandwiches on a buffet table, one platter holding meat and egg sandwiches, another varieties of fish, another assorted cheese combinations. Count on four or five sandwiches per guest—they are so tempting, it's almost impossible not to go back again and again. The garnishes are intrinsic to the sandwiches; anything else, other than a frill of watercress or parsley on the edges of the platters, is lily-gilding.

All this highly flavored food is thirst-producing. Foamy Danish beer is just right, or icy glasses of aquavit. Finish up with flaky Danish pastry (the Danish modestly call it Wienerbrod, attributing it to the Viennese), a basket of fruit, and lots of coffee.

Most smørrebrød combinations go well on a substantial bread, such as big slices of pumpernickel or rye, although some of the less demanding flavors can be put together on a sturdy white bread, such as vienna. As a first step, lightly butter each slice of bread. When you're making these sandwiches, be generous with both the foundation food and the garnish, covering the bread to the edges. Here are some examples of classic Danish smørrebrød.

Smoked salmon–scrambled egg: Place enough slices of fresh smoked salmon on the bread to cover it totally. Add a ribbon of cold scrambled eggs, spooned diagonally across. Garnish the top with finely chopped chives.
Salami–raw egg: Cover the bread with many thin slices of salami sausage. Place a thick onion ring in the center and slip a raw egg yolk into it.
Samso cheese: Cover the bread with thick slices of samso cheese. Garnish the cheese with sliced fresh cucumber.

Salami–onion: Cover the bread with lettuce, the lettuce with slices of salami and onion rings.

Pâté de foie–cucumber: Spread the pâté on the bread and top it with tomato and cucumber slices.

Deviled ham–olive: Spread the bread with deviled ham and top it with four or more pitted whole ripe olives.

Danish brie: Cover the buttered bread with three or four thick slices of brie cheese.

Shrimp: Cover the bread completely with a layer of ice-cold cooked shrimp. Garnish the shrimp with paper-thin lemon slices.

Danish blue: Cover the bread with thin overlapping slices of Danish blue cheese.

Danish blue plus: Spread the bread thickly with softened Danish blue cheese. Hollow out the cheese in the center and slip a raw egg yolk into the well.

Danish caviar: Center a slice of buttered bread on a large lettuce leaf. Spread the bread with Danish caviar; top the caviar with chopped hard-cooked egg white, a thin lemon slice, and sprigs of parsley.

Danish ham: Cover the buttered bread with a few slices of Danish ham, a layer of Italian Salad (see Index), and a sprinkle of snipped watercress.

Boiled ham: Center the bread on a large lettuce leaf. Cover it with sliced boiled ham. Decorate the ham with sliced peaches (canned or fresh) and glacé cherry.

Ham and egg: Cover the bread completely with thin-sliced ham. Fry an egg slowly in butter just until the white is set. Slide it, sizzling hot, onto the ham; garnish the top with watercress and a tomato slice. Serve this one warm.

Ham and asparagus: Center the bread on large lettuce leaf. Cover it with sliced boiled ham. Place asparagus spears diagonally across the ham and top all with a continuous strip of tomato peel.

Ham and cheese: Place a lettuce leaf on the bread slice. Top it with a large slice of ham and a large slice of cheese. Garnish it with tomato slices and watercress.

Ham and scrambled egg: Cover the bread with sliced ham. Place a scrambled egg on one half of the bread, sliced tomatoes on the other half. Garnish it with watercress sprigs.

Ham and egg plus: Place a lettuce leaf on the bread slice. Top it with a slice of boiled ham. Add a layer of scrambled eggs sprinkled with chopped chives.

Canadian bacon–tomato: On the bread, combine slices of Canadian bacon, tomato, and sprigs of watercress.

Zesty Canadian bacon: Cover the bread with a lettuce leaf, then with sliced Canadian-style bacon. Decorate the bacon with a diagonal strip of shredded horseradish and top all with a strip of tomato peel and a sprig of parsley.

Braunschweiger: Cover the bread with a lettuce leaf, then with two slices of braunschweiger. Garnish the top with julienne swiss cheese, two half slices of crisp bacon, and sliced olives.

Cocktail sausage: Place a layer of cocktail sausages on buttered bread. Place a strip of crisp bacon diagonally across them. Top them with sautéed mushroom caps speared with food picks.

Cocktail eggs I: Place the bread on a large lettuce leaf. Cover it with cocktail sausages and decorate it with a strip of scrambled eggs topped by parsley sprigs.

Cocktail eggs II: Place a lettuce leaf on the bread. Halve a hard-cooked egg lengthwise; place both halves face down on the center of the leaf. Top each half with a cocktail sausage speared with a food pick.

Beef béarnaise: Cover the bread with slices of cold roast beef and garnish them with béarnaise sauce.

Boiled beef: Place slices of boiled beef on the bread. Place a slice of tomato in the center, chopped pickle at one end, and shredded horseradish at the other.

Beef—egg: Cover the bread with slices of cold roast beef. Sauté onion slices in butter until they are lightly browned; spread them over the beef and top them with a fried egg.

Danish tartar: Cover the bread with a layer of raw ground beef. Top it with an onion ring; place a hard-cooked egg yolk in the center. Garnish the top with capers and chopped raw onion.

Smoked eel: Cut the eel in pieces about the size of the bread slice. Skin and bone the eel slices and place them on the bread. Top them with chive-sprinkled scrambled eggs.

Tomato and egg: On one half of a slice of bread, place slices of hard-cooked egg. On the other half, place slices of tomato. Garnish the top with onion rings and watercress.

Hans Andersen: Cover the bread with slices of liver paste. Decorate the top with crisscrossed slices of crisp bacon and garnish it with tomato slices, grated horseradish, and a strip of jellied consommé.

Liver pâté: Cover the buttered bread with a thick slice of good liver pâté. Top the pâté with thin slices of fried bacon. Sauté sliced mushrooms in butter, season them with salt and pepper, and heap them generously on the bacon.

Lobster salad: Mix small pieces of cold lobster and cooked or canned (and well-drained) asparagus with mayonnaise. Place a large lettuce leaf on the buttered bread and spread the lobster mixture on it. Garnish the top with asparagus tips.

Anchovies and eggs: Slice two hard-cooked eggs and layer the slices in rows on a buttered slice of bread. Cover the eggs with anchovies and sliced tomatoes and garnish the top with watercress.

The local way

Another handsome, delicious open-face sandwich meal that serves well for entertaining combines good old American pot roast with a jellied two-tone garnish that is a triumph of both looks and taste. Because this entire meal is served cold, you can make everything ahead of time—cook the beef two days before the party, make the jellied relish the day before. Assemble the bread-and-meat part of the sandwiches before the company comes and slip a slice of relish on each just before serving. Beer is good with these sturdy sandwiches: Accompany them with a big salad of

Opposite: Smørrebrød

mixed greens with sliced hard-cooked eggs, strips of cheese, and croutons. Top off the meal with a homemade fudge cake (make this the day
before, too) and a big pot of coffee or, if it's very hot, iced coffee or tea.

JEWEL-TOP BEEF SANDWICHES   12 servings

for pot roast:

2 tablespoons cooking oil
5 pounds beef bottom round
2 carrots, scraped and quartered
2 onions, quartered
2 stalks celery, quartered

2 cloves garlic, minced
1/2 cup chopped parsley
1 bay leaf
1 tablespoon salt

for red relish layer:

2 tablespoons (envelopes)
   unflavored gelatin
1 cup tomato juice, divided
1 cup pan gravy from pot roast
2 tablespoons tomato paste
1 tablespoon prepared mustard

2 teaspoons onion juice
3 drops hot pepper sauce
Salt
1 cup chopped celery
1/3 cup chopped sweet pickle

for golden relish layer:

2 tablespoons (envelopes)
   unflavored gelatin
1/2 cup dill pickle juice
1/2 teaspoon turmeric
1 cup pan gravy from pot roast
1/2 cup mayonnaise
2 tablespoons prepared
   horseradish, drained

Salt and white pepper
2 tablespoons chopped chives
1 cup chopped cucumber (seeds
   and pulp removed)
1/2 cup chopped dill pickle

To prepare pot roast: In a dutch oven, heat cooking oil. Brown pot roast on all
sides. Add carrots, onions, celery, garlic, parsley, bay leaf, and salt. Add 2 cups
water. Bring to a boil. Cover; reduce heat and simmer until fork tender, about
3 hours. Remove meat and refrigerate. Strain pan gravy and refrigerate.

To prepare red relish: Soften gelatin in 1/2 cup of the tomato juice. Measure pan
gravy from pot roast; add water as necessary to make 2 cups liquid. To 1 cup
of this liquid, add softened gelatin, remaining 1/2 cup tomato juice, tomato paste,
mustard, onion juice, and hot pepper sauce. Stir over medium heat until gelatin
is dissolved. Cool. Season to taste with salt. Refrigerate until it is the consistency
of unbeaten egg white. Add celery and sweet pickle. Rinse an 8- x 5- x 3-inch
loaf pan in cold water. Pour in red relish. Refrigerate.

To prepare golden relish: Soften gelatin in pickle juice; stir in turmeric. Place
remaining cup pan gravy in a saucepan; add softened gelatin. Stir over medium

heat until gelatin is dissolved. Cool. Stir in mayonnaise and horseradish; season to taste with salt and white pepper. Refrigerate until it is the consistency of unbeaten egg white. Stir in chives, cucumber, and dill pickle. Pour over congealed layer of red relish in loaf pan. Refrigerate overnight.

To make sandwiches: Lightly butter 12 slices of italian or vienna bread. Place overlapping slices of pot roast on the bread, and season them lightly with salt. Just before serving, unmold the jellied relish loaf. Place a ½-inch slice of the loaf over the meat on each bread slice. Place the sandwiches on individual plates or on a large platter or tray and surround them with watercress sprigs.

Good sandwich sense

Whenever you serve a sandwich—to the children, as a family meal, to guests—never make the mistake of thinking of it as "just" a sandwich. Think positive. Make it a very good sandwich, serve it attractively, and bring it to the table proudly. It is a production and it deserves deferential treatment.

Garnishing Salads

Most salads are, by their very nature, good to look at. (The only kind that might be less than so is the potato salad offered for sale by some delicatessens—cold white lumps held together by cold white goo.) Salad ingredients are beautiful in themselves. The greens alone range in color from pale tender to dark assertive, in shape from smooth flat to stand-up curly, in size from minute to plate-covering, in texture from buttery to crisp, in flavor from bland to bitey.

The woman who offered as one of the reasons she left her husband that he wanted a tossed salad with dinner every evening of their married life simply had no imagination. Considering all the possible additions to such a salad, all the possible ways to dress it, all the possible combinations of greens, and the infinite permutations on those combinations, she could have served a different tossed salad every night, and saved their marriage! And if she could have coaxed her husband away from tossed salads and offered him mixed salads, composed salads, molded salads, soup salads (yes, think about fruit soups and gazpacho, to name just two), cooked-ingredient salads, even main-dish salads, their blissful wedded state could have stretched into eternity.

Cool green thoughts

"Salad" and "iceberg lettuce" are not necessarily synonyms. To be sure, good sturdy (and sometimes, unfortunately, almost tasteless) iceberg has a place in the salad scheme of things. But there's a wider world of greens waiting to find a home in your salad bowl, to make a far tastier, handsomer salad than iceberg alone. A salad of several greens—different flavors, different textures, different shades—can be, as well as a great taste experience, so fine to look at that it is, by itself, a garnish to grace the meal.

Here is a selection to help you think green:

iceberg lettuce (don't count it out entirely)—big, firm heads, pale- to medium-green; mild flavor

bibb lettuce—tiny heads, richly green; tender and succulent

boston (also called butter) lettuce—small heads, pale yellow-green; tender and buttery

leaf (also called salad bowl) lettuce—big, raggedy heads with ruffle-edge leaves, medium- to dark-green; keeps its crispness (for that reason, fine for wilted-lettuce salads)

redhead lettuce—like leaf, except that the tops of its leaves shade to rusty-red

romaine—long-leafed, elegant and crisp; center leaves pale, outer ones dark; the backbone of caesar salad; boat-shaped leaves excellent to fill with other salads

escarole—like a shorter-leaf, curly-edge romaine; medium green; stronger flavor than romaine

chicory—dark green leaves with frilly edges; strong, sometimes bitter flavor

chinese cabbage—long, frilled, yellow-green leaves; flavor mild, halfway between celery and cabbage

watercress—comes as a bound-together bouquet of sprigs; small, deep-green leaves; flavor pungent and peppery

parsley—another bouquet of sprigs; crinkly-crisp, dark green; assertive flavor

belgian endive—small heads of pale spears with light yellow-green edges; very crisp; mildly bitter flavor; slice in thin rounds or use smaller spears whole

spinach—deep green leaves; crinkly or smooth, depending on where it's grown; young leaves are tender, sweetly flavored

For the pathfinder

There are other greens, not as commonly used as those listed, that make splendid additions to a mixed salad. In using these, choose only the youngest, tenderest plants—old ones are likely to be tough and strong-flavored. In any case, these have more flavor, usually more bite, than the general run of salad greens, so try them judiciously, torn or snipped into smallish pieces. They include dandelion greens (a wonderful way to clean up the lawn in the spring), mustard greens, turnip greens, beet greens, kale (with all of these, use only the thinner leaf parts, discarding stems and ribs), arugola, celery leaves and nasturtium leaves (deliciously peppery).

Green, but not greens

There are many other possible green additions to a tossed salad that can add zest, texture and flavor contrast, and—never forget it—beauty. Long, thin slivers of scallion, including some of the tops. All the cabbages—young and tender new cabbage, crinkly savoy, pale and mild nappa. Celery and fennel slices. Artichoke hearts (frozen, cooked, or from cans or jars). Bean sprouts and alfalfa sprouts. Snipped chives. Thin rounds or spears of cucumber and zucchini. Fresh-from-the-garden (yours or the greengrocer's) herbs, such as dill, basil, tarragon, mint, chervil, coriander, and summer savory.

Make now, toss later

To achieve optimum eye appeal for your mixed green salad, prepare your choice of greens and combine them in the salad bowl. (A shallow, wide bowl is better than a deep, narrow one—it shows off your pretty salad better and, when the salad is tossed, all the delightful surprises you've added don't sink to the bottom and get lost.) Cover the salad and refrigerate it until just before you're ready to serve. Then arrange on top of the bed of greens whatever garnish you're going to add—for flavor, for texture, for substance, or just for pretty—in an attractive pattern. Bring the salad and its dressing to the table separately and then, when everyone's eye is pleased and appetite whetted, dress, toss, and serve it immediately. Besides the bonus of beauty, you'll achieve maximum crispness this way —a great virtue in the taste of a salad.

What can you use to make the attractively arranged garnish? Almost anything that leaps to your mind. Try these, separately or in any number of combinations, to get you started:

cubes or slivers of cheese (any kind)
small pretzel sticks or crumbled larger pretzels
plain or flavored croutons, packaged or homemade
sliced raw mushrooms
shredded carrots, or a mound of carrot curls
sliced or shredded white or red radishes
bite-size dry cereal
nuts (any kind), plain, salted, or toasted

coarsely crumbled corn chips or potato chips
canned (drained) kidney beans, white beans, or chick peas
paper-thin strips of turnip, rutabaga, or beet
crumbled crisp bacon
meat or poultry (any kind) in chunks or strips
packaged stuffing mix
canned or packaged chinese noodles
rings of sweet white or red onion
broken cheese crackers

paper-thin rings of sweet red or
  green pepper
sliced water chestnuts
packaged coconut chips
pickle slices or chunks
whole or halved grapes
avocado slices or chunks
canned french-fried onions
pimiento slivers
tomato slices, chunks, or halved
  cherry tomatoes

chopped or sliced hard-cooked egg
plain or seasoned popcorn
orange or grapefruit sections
sliced bamboo shoots
sliced stuffed or pitted green, ripe,
  or green-ripe olives
anchovy fillets
skinless and boneless sardines

Salads with individuality

All salads don't come to the table in bowls. Some arrive on individual serving plates, suitably garnished. Such one-on-one servings of salad can be anything from a ring of pineapple and a dab of cottage cheese to the splendid unctuousness of hearts of palm. Whatever its chief ingredients, each salad needs two components to make it complete: greenery of some sort underneath it and a garnish of some sort beside or on top of it. The greenery can be any of the greens (plus grape leaves) from the preceding greens list.

As for the garnish, small vegetable shapes (close relatives of the larger, main-dish "flowers") work well on single portions. They can be—should be—made in advance, and will wait accommodatingly for their special moment.

Scallion ruffles: Trim off the root end and all but 2 inches of the tops of slim scallions. Starting at the root end, make a cut through the stalk down to where the green begins to show; turn the scallion and make a second cut at a right angle to the first. Chill the scallions in ice water so the ruffles will separate and curl.

Carrot curls: Peel a carrot. With a vegetable parer, cut long, very thin slices from it, top to bottom. Roll each slice around your finger and fasten the curl with a food pick. Chill the curls in ice water; remove the picks before serving.

Carrot pleats: Cut the carrots into thin slices as above. Thread each slice onto a food pick, accordion-style. Chill them in ice water and remove the picks, before serving.

Carrot whirligigs: Insert the point of a short-bladed paring knife into a peeled, whole carrot, cutting at a slight angle to, but not through, the center; turn the carrot slowly, making a long, continuous spiral cut around the carrot. Chill the whirligigs in ice water until they open.

Radish roses: Cut the top of the root end off each radish; leave a few green leaves on each stem end. Using a sharp-pointed paring knife, cut four or five thin petals around each radish, leaving a little red between petals. Chill the radishes in ice water until the petals open.

Radish accordions: Cut long red radishes crosswise, from the top almost to the bottom, in eight to ten narrow slices. Chill the radishes in ice water until the accordions fan out.

Radish pompons: Slice off the root end, retaining a few of the leaves of large radishes. Using a sharp knife, make a row of cuts ½-inch deep, slicing from the root end almost to the stem end. Turn the radish and

make a similar series of cuts at right angles to first series. Chill the radishes in ice water until the petals spread.

Radish whirlarounds: Trim both ends from the radish, cutting one end flat so that the radish will stand up. Cut five vertical slits, evenly spaced, around the radish. Cut five 1/8-inch-thick slices from another radish. Insert the slices in the slits of the first radish. Decorate the top with a tiny parsley sprig.

Cherry-tomato flowers: Using the tip of a sharp knife, make four cuts, just skin deep, halfway down the sides of firm cherry tomatoes. Drop the tomatoes into boiling water for 1 minute; plunge them at once into cold water. Using the knife tip, carefully peel back the sections between the cuts, halfway down the sides, to make petals. Garnish the tops with a little sieved hard-cooked egg yolk.

Cucumber twists: Using the tines of a fork, score the outside of an unpeeled cucumber from one end to the other heavily enough to penetrate the peel. Cut the cucumber into 1/8-inch-thick slices. Cut from the center to the edge of each slice; grasp the edges of the cut gently and twist them in opposite directions.

Any of these vegetable garnishes, singly or in twos or threes, alone or combined with olives or pickles, perks up the looks and the taste of single-serving salad plates, or they may be used to surround a mound of potato or macaroni or similar salad, or to decorate its bowl or that of a simple tossed salad.

Stuff it, fill it

Small stalks of celery or blades of belgian endive, or chunks of larger celery stalks or of fennel, can all be stuffed with any savory mixture to add contrast and substance to individual salad plates. Bland or sharp or smoky cheeses, softened with a little milk or cream, alone or mixed with snipped chives, chopped olives, or chopped nuts, make tasty fillings. So do pastes of cream cheese combined with mashed anchovies or sardines, or with finely chopped ham or canned deviled ham, or mashed liver sausage or canned liver pâté. Or use one of the following stuffed-vegetable garnishes.

Cucumber wheels: Peel, halve crosswise, and core (use an apple corer) medium-size cucumbers. Fill the hollowed centers with softened cream cheese seasoned with chives and/or finely minced shrimp, or with softened smoke-flavored cheese. Refrigerate the cucumbers until the cheese is firm; cut them into 3/4-inch-thick slices.

Mushroom mounds: Wipe medium-size mushrooms clean with a damp cloth. Twist out the stems and, using a spoon, hollow out the caps slightly. Mince the stems and combine them with softened cream cheese seasoned with celery seed and anchovy paste; or combine them with shredded jack

Opposite: Salad greens—romaine, spinach, zucchini, chives—and red onions

cheese and shredded salami, moistened with a little cream. Fill the caps with the mixture, mounding it high.

Blue endive wheels: Cut off the stem ends of endive heads; separate blades. Combine cream and blue cheeses, half and half (moisten with a little sour cream if necessary). Spread a layer of the cheese mixture on each endive blade. Reassemble the heads of endive, starting with the smallest blades. Wrap the heads tightly in foil or plastic wrap and refrigerate them. Just before serving, cut the heads into ½-inch-thick slices.

Celery rosettes (see Index) are another superior stuffed-vegetable garnish for salads or individual salad plates.

The cook as artist

Composed salads, in the making, are exceedingly satisfying to the artist that lurks in the soul of every cook; as ornaments for a party meal, particularly a buffet, they justify every moment (surprisingly, not as much time as they look to have taken) that is spent on them. And in the eating, they are gustatory delights.

What's a composed salad? A handsome, well-thought-out arrangement of any of dozens of ingredients, in good looks/taste combinations—a kind of edible free-style art form, one of the high points of the craft of making food beautiful. Generally, "the bigger the better" is a composed-salad guideline—one of the reasons they're so good for large-crowd buffets. Use your imagination in choosing the container. A big platter is fine. So is a tray of almost any shape. Offbeat containers work well, too—a giant-size plant saucer; a large, shallow basket (line the bottom with plastic wrap); the bottom third sliced from a big pumpkin; a Mexican metate (the stone on which corn is ground to make the flour for tortillas); or almost anything else that comes to mind and to hand that is large, shallow, and offers a reasonably flat surface.

Here are some compositions to try—then let your imagination guide you. In all cases, be sure to provide serving utensils so guests can help themselves.

Salade Niçoise: Make this excellent Mediterranean main-dish salad in any quantity, depending on the number of guests. Line the container you've chosen with leaves of salad bowl, leaf, or redhead lettuce. Place a mound of high-quality, solid-pack canned tuna in the center if the container is round, at one end if it is oval or rectangular. Arrange around it, or radiating out from it, or in any other pattern that appeals to you, separate mounds of chilled green beans, cooked tender-crisp; sliced chilled cooked new potatoes; celery, thinly sliced on the diagonal; thin rings of sweet green pepper; thin slices of red onion; and peeled cherry tomatoes. Arrange quarters of hard-cooked egg, each topped with an anchovy fillet, among the mounds. Combine dried rosemary and dried thyme and sprinkle the vegetables with the mixture. Then sprinkle them with thinly sliced scallions, including some of the green tops. Liberally scatter greek- or italian-style ripe olives over the composition. In a separate bowl or in a cruet, serve a garlicky olive oil–wine vinegar dressing, sparked with dijon mustard.

Tricolor salad: Choose a long, rather narrow container; line it with leaves of boston lettuce. Arrange thin slices of cooked beet, peeled orange, and bermuda onion as your fancy dictates—in rows of alternating slices, in separate rows, however you choose. Provide a separate bowl of sour cream to use as dressing.

Garden bounty: Plan to make this only when fresh basil and garden-fresh beefsteak tomatoes are in season. Line the container with watercress. Arrange tomato slices in an attractive pattern, overlapping them slightly. Combine three parts salt, one part coarsely ground black pepper, and one part granulated sugar. Sprinkle the tomatoes with the mixture and let them stand at room temperature for 15 minutes. Sprinkle the tomatoes thickly with chopped fresh basil and drizzle olive or salad oil lightly over them. For many, the salad will require no further dressing; you might provide a cruet of red-wine vinegar for those who want to add a touch of tartness.

Whole-meal Scandinavian salad: Have ready hot cooked, peeled new potatoes, and a dressing made of one part cider vinegar to two parts salad oil. In a mixing bowl, place a layer of potato slices. Sprinkle them with salt, pepper, and paprika. Strew thinly sliced scallions over the slices and drizzle them with some of the dressing. Repeat the layering until all the ingredients are used. Refrigerate the salad. Combine softened cream cheese with chopped fresh dill; spread the mixture on slices of smoked salmon. Roll the salmon up, jelly-roll fashion, and secure each roll with a food pick. Refrigerate them. Cut cooked ham into strips and edam cheese into strips of comparable size. Refrigerate them separately. Hard-cook enough eggs to provide at least one half for each diner. Peel and halve the eggs; place the yolks in a bowl and mash them. To the yolks add salt, cayenne pepper, and dry mustard to taste; moisten the mixture with a little sour cream. Mound the mixture in the whites and refrigerate the eggs. Make radish pompons (see Index) and refrigerate them in ice water. At serving time, line a container of your choice with greens. Drain the potato mixture in a colander. Mound the mixture in the center or at one end of the container and sprinkle it with drained capers. Cut the salmon rolls into ¼-inch-thick slices. Arrange the salmon-roll slices and the ham and cheese strips separately on the greens. Intersperse the deviled-egg halves and radish pompons, and finish the platter with long, thin strips of dill pickle. Serve mayonnaise separately.

Dressed-up fruit salads

Any season of the year is fruit salad season. During cold weather, citrus fruit, melons, and other fruit brought from warmer climates taste like summer to winter-tired palates. And when the weather turns warm and the succession of local fruit begins, there's nothing quite as refreshing as a fruit salad. Such salads, nicely garnished, and with something pretty and substantial on the side, can be a delicious main dish when heat makes appetites favor light, cool-seeming food. Any time of the year, a fruit combination can double as both salad and dessert. Good to taste, good to look at, versatile—what more could you ask?

Simple one- or two-fruit salads compose best on individual salad plates. Those made of several fruits, particularly for more than three or four people, compose beautifully on platters, trays, or large plates. Or fruits can take to the salad bowl, by themselves or combined with greens. The tender, more delicately flavored greens partner better with fruit than the strong- or bitter-flavored ones, both as bases for composed salads and in combination with fruit in a bowl of mixed salad.

Fruit singles and doubles

Juicy spears of fresh pineapple, each rolled in chopped mint, make a delightful individual salad bedded on bibb lettuce. Or combine pineapple and whole strawberries in an attractive pattern and sprinkle them with sliced macadamia nuts. Peel a honeyball or cantaloupe, halve it, scoop out the seeds, and cut it into rings. Place the rings on individual plates lined with butter lettuce, pile the centers with berries, with grapes and berries, or with berries and pineapple chunks; nest small cream cheese balls, rolled in finely chopped peanuts, among the fruit. Or alternate pale yellow grapefruit segments with yellow-green avocado sections on tender young spinach leaves for the coolest-looking salad ever. With such salads, offer a dressing of half-and-half mayonnaise and sour cream, or half-and-half honey and lime juice. Or try mayonnaise with grated lemon peel stirred into it.

Peaches, pears, and apricots—fresh in season, canned when out of season—take kindly to having their centers filled with neat little balls of any number of savory mixtures. A combination of cream and blue cheese, rolled in chopped pistachios, goes well with any of these fruit flavors. So do small portions of salmon or tuna salad. Peaches and ham salad have an affinity for one another. With pears, try cubes of sharp cheddar rolled in paprika; with apricots, cubes of monterey jack rolled in snipped chives.

Icy cold peach or pear halves topped with hot shrimp balls are an unbeatable flavor–texture–temperature combination and make a great addition to a party buffet. The shrimp balls can be made in advance and reheated in a 375°F. oven just before serving. In fact, they can be made far ahead of time, frozen, thawed in the refrigerator the day of the party, and oven-heated just before going to the table.

SHRIMP BALLS   28 balls

4 cups fresh bread crumbs	½ teaspoon ground coriander
½ cup milk	½ teaspoon salt
Vegetable oil, divided	¼ teaspoon pepper
1 pound shrimp, shelled and deveined	4 eggs, divided
	1½ tablespoons chopped parsley
2 tablespoons minced onion	¾ cup fine dry bread crumbs

Combine fresh bread crumbs and milk; reserve. In a skillet, heat 1 tablespoon oil; add shrimp, onion, coriander, salt, and pepper. Sauté just until shrimp turn pink. In container of blender, chop shrimp mixture, a little at a time; add to bread crumb mixture. Beat 2 eggs well; add to shrimp mixture. Add parsley and combine well. Cool. Heat vegetable oil for deep frying to 375°F. Beat remaining eggs. Drop shrimp mixture, a tablespoon at a time, into dry bread crumbs, then into beaten eggs, then again into bread crumbs. Deep fry about 3 minutes, or until golden brown. Drain on paper towels.

Salad garnishes, sweet and savory

Blue-cheese cherries (see Index) or nut-stuffed dates or prunes make a different-taste accompaniment for almost any fruit salad. Slices of kiwi are beautiful and delicious. Or try orange slices, each topped with a dab of sour cream and sprinkled with brown sugar, as a garnish. Kumquat flowers are especially nice for zesty taste and chewy texture. Use either the fresh or the preserved fruit.

Kumquat flowers: Using a knife or scissors, cut each fruit into six or eight sections, cutting downward about three-quarters of the way to the bottom, so that the sections will fan out. Spread the sections apart and remove a portion of the pulp. Tuck half a maraschino or candied or minted cherry in the center.

Lilies made of golden or pale-green melon also decorate a fruit salad nicely, and add an extra flavor dimension.

Melon lilies: Peel a small cantaloupe or honeydew melon; cut it in half crosswise and remove the seeds. Cut it into very thin rings and make one cut through each ring. Roll the ring into a cone shape and secure it with a food pick—the result will resemble a calla lily. Put a touch of very finely slivered orange, lemon, or lime peel in the center of each cone. Use the cones singly or in clusters of three.

Home-toasted seeds make an unusual sprinkle for almost any kind of salad. Hull pumpkin, sunflower, or squash seeds and toast them over low heat in a skillet in which you've melted a little butter. Or toast sesame seeds, without butter, in a moderate oven, spread on a baking sheet.

Artichokes mimosa are a delicious addition to a chicken, seafood, or meat salad, and add a just-right touch of decoration, too.

Artichokes mimosa: Toss cooked quartered artichoke bottoms in french dressing. Into a bowl, sieve hard-cooked eggs (both yolks and whites) and add about half as much finely chopped parsley. Season the mixture to taste with salt and white pepper. Dip one edge of each artichoke quarter in the egg mixture.

For fruit salads—especially those you'd like to entice children to eat—marshmallows are an excellent garnish. Sprinkle the small ones over the salad or fold them into a mixture of fruits. Or make marshmallow flowers (see Index), using the larger candies.

And to go with the salad

Virtually all salads, particularly those that form the nucleus of the meal, need some sort of bread or rolls to complement them. Rolls need not necessarily be white, not necessarily cloverleaf. Expand your horizons to include pillowy wholewheat rolls; sturdy, smooth-crust pumpernickel or rye rolls; egg-rich little parkerhouse rolls; and hard french rolls. Choose bran muffins, berry muffins, corn muffins, or corn bread (great with honey butter). Try tea breads—banana, orange, nut, cinnamon, molasses-oatmeal, date-nut. They are even better when sliced whisper thin and sandwiched with cream cheese. If you're faced with unexpected company, the salad you put together from what was in the cupboard and the refrigerator (that's one of the splendid things about salad) doesn't have to go to the table naked as long as there is a package of melba toast, rusks, zwieback, crisp crackers, corn chips, or potato chips on the pantry shelf. Or, if there's time (under 30 minutes from the thought to the finished product), whip up a batch of corn bread or muffins or biscuits from a mix.

Bread calls for butter

There's nothing wrong with neat little pats of butter, cut from a quarter-pound stick, except that they have no personality. Butter balls do, so do butter curls and butter molds. For butter balls you need special paddles, two of them, made of wood with ridges running their length. It takes a bit of practice, but once you get the hang of it you can turn out butter balls with speed and virtuosity. Instructions come with the paddles.

A butter curler is a metal tool, shaped something like a long-legged question mark, with teeth on the rounded part. Drawn over a smooth surface of butter, it produces handsome striated curls—with a little practice, you'll use it like an expert. Ballers and curlers can be purchased at hardware or specialty shops. So can butter molds, into which butter is packed, then unmolded bearing any one of a dozen pretty designs. All these fancy-shape butters can be made in advance and can wait, in ice water, in the refrigerator until serving time.

Sandwich fingers, sandwich shapes

Any salad is the better for a sandwich or two to keep it company, but such sandwiches should be mild and simple, to grace the salad rather than compete with it. Finger sandwiches are made of two paper-thin bread slices with an uncomplicated filling, the crusts trimmed, and the sandwiches cut into three or four lengths. Watercress, parsley, thin cucumber slices, alfalfa or bean sprouts on buttered bread make traditional sandwiches of this kind. Plain thin bread (again, it doesn't always have to be white) sandwiched with a generous amount of flavored butter, sweet or savory, can be cut into fingers or any shape that suits you, such as small triangles or diamonds or—using cookie cutters—rounds or stars or, if you like, playing card pips or (for the children) animal shapes.

For all these sandwiches, whipped butter is lighter and spreads more easily than the regular kind. You can buy whipped butter, sweet or salted, or you can easily and more economically make it at home. As is often true with a homemade product, it's heavenly—much better than the store-bought variety—and not difficult to make.

WHIPPED BUTTER   two 1-pound containers

1 pound butter, sweet or salted, at   *1 egg*
room temperature   *¼ cup cold heavy cream*

In the bowl of an electric mixer, combine butter and egg. Beat at low speed until blended, then at high speed 5 minutes. Add cream; combine at low speed, then beat at high speed 10 to 15 minutes, or until very light and fluffy. Place in two airtight 1-pound containers. Refrigerate.

Delicious as a spread for bread, this whipped butter can be seasoned divers ways to be used in simple sandwiches. To ¾ cup of whipped butter, add any of the following:

½ cup grated cheddar cheese, plus ⅛ teaspoon dry mustard

3 tablespoons prepared horseradish, drained

3 tablespoons chopped chutney

2 teaspoons curry powder (or to taste)

¼ cup finely chopped parsley, mint, or basil leaves, plus ½ teaspoon lemon juice

1 tablespoon lemon juice, plus 1 tablespoon grated lemon peel

1 tablespoon lime juice, plus 2 teaspoons grated lime peel

1 tablespoon orange juice, plus 2 tablespoons grated orange peel

2 tablespoons confectioners sugar, plus ½ teaspoon cinnamon or ¼ teaspoon mace

3 tablespoons finely chopped walnuts, pecans, filberts, pistachios, or cashews

¼ cup snipped chives

¼ cup finely snipped fresh tarragon, plus ½ teaspoon lemon juice

2 tablespoons caraway or toasted sesame seed

1 tablespoon anchovy paste, plus ¼ teaspoon lemon juice

2 tablespoons chili sauce, plus 3 drops hot pepper sauce

2 tablespoons catsup, plus ¼ teaspoon lemon juice and ⅛ teaspoon cayenne pepper

1 tablespoon onion juice

2 tablespoons grated parmesan or romano cheese

1 teaspoon garlic juice, plus ¼ teaspoon lemon juice and ⅛ teaspoon celery seed (for dark, dense-texture breads)

1 teaspoon worcestershire sauce

4 skinless, boneless sardines, mashed

2 tablespoons well-drained india relish, plus ½ teaspoon onion powder

1 tablespoon confectioners sugar, plus 1 teaspoon vanilla extract

7 or 8 ripe strawberries, mashed, plus 1 teaspoon confectioners sugar

20 ripe raspberries, mashed, plus ⅛ teaspoon lemon juice and 1 tablespoon confectioners sugar

There is, of course, no law that says these wonderful butters must be used only on sandwiches that accompany salads. Try the sweet ones on hot toast, or any of the savory ones on hot toast topped with a poached or soft-scrambled egg. Or have any one of them, sweet or savory, on a thin slice of bread or toast to serve as that little something extra with a midafternoon cup of coffee or tea.

Cups, baskets, holders of all sorts
Many salads, particularly damp ones and certainly damp ones that are

Opposite: Individual fruit salads—honeydew rings, green grapes, blueberries, pineapple chunks, cream cheese balls rolled in nuts

going to share a plate with other food, as at a buffet, are best served in some sort of container that will not only keep them neat, but also enhance their good looks. Small bowls or cups—even paper ones—will do, but hollowed out fruit or vegetable containers are infinitely more attractive and some offer the lagniappe of being edible themselves after their contents are consumed. Small containers can be used to hold salad dressings, large ones to hold a whole salad. In general, the logical rule is to use fruit containers for fruit salads and vegetable containers for vegetable and meat–vegetable combinations, but like any rule, this one exists only to be taken exception to. Use whatever container seems right and looks right to you.

Apple cups: Choose a big red apple; do not peel it. Using an apple corer, take out the core, starting at the stem end; do not cut all the way through to the bottom. Hollow the apple out, using a spoon, or cut it into wedges, down to ¼ inch of the bottom. Brush it with lemon juice to prevent darkening.

Artichoke cups: Cut off the top third of raw artichokes, scoop out the chokes. Cook them in acidulated water until they are tender crisp and drain them upside down. Spread the leaves to fill the cups with salad or dressing.

Artichoke saucers: Canned, already-cooked artichoke bottoms can hold individual dressings of the mayonnaise or sour cream types.

Egg cups: Hard-cook and shell the eggs. Halve them crosswise and remove the yolks. Using a sharp, pointed knife, cut the edges of the whites in a sawtooth pattern. If necessary, cut a thin slice off the bottom of the egg half so it will stand up. As a salad garnish, these cups can be filled with almost any mixture you like, but they are particularly useful as holders for dressing for individual composed cooked-vegetable salads, with the yolks used as the basis of the dressing. Mash the yolks thoroughly, add vegetable oil and lemon juice (for delicately flavored vegetables) or olive oil and wine vinegar (for sturdier flavors), a few drops of onion or garlic juice, salt, and cayenne pepper. Spoon the mixture into the egg-white cups, and place one on each salad plate.

Citrus-fruit cups: Lime, lemon, orange, or grapefruit cups (see Index) serve well as holders for dressing, or for small portions of salad. For example, an orange cup is an excellent container for orange–cabbage slaw. If you like, use a whole fruit rather than a half for each cup and retain a strip of peel over the top when you carve, thereby creating a basket shape.

Melon bowls or baskets: Cut a cantaloupe or small honeydew in half for individual servings, or use larger melons to hold salads for several people. Remove the seeds and some of the pulp—in chunks or in balls, with a melon baller—to use in the salad, or for dessert on another occasion. Leave a shell sturdy enough to stand, however. You may serrate or scallop the edges or not, as you prefer. Fill the melon with ham, chicken, or seafood salad, or any kind of mixed-fruit salad. If you like, use a whole melon for each container, leaving a strip over the top for a handle, to make a melon basket. If you'd like a melon bowl or basket in which to serve fruit salad to a large number of people, use a watermelon, hollowing it in the same way and retaining part of the meat of the melon for the salad. Such a hollowed-out watermelon makes an excellent punch bowl for al fresco parties, too.

Tomato cups and pepper cups (see Index) can also be used for individual servings of salad. Peppers make attractive baskets—use a whole pepper, large end down, retaining a top strip for a handle. Be content with cups of tomato, however. They don't lend themselves to being handled baskets.

Making it in a mold

Fruit or vegetable side-dish salad molds and meat, fish, or poultry main-dish molded salads are excellent ways to serve salad with a difference that is both delicious to taste and delightful to look at. Such salads, side-dish or main-dish, can be prepared in individual molds to serve one person or in larger ones up to a size that will satisfy the hunger of a large party of diligent eaters.

Shops selling gourmet cooking utensils offer an array of molds in a multitude of shapes and sizes, some of them exceedingly handsome in themselves and designed to produce equally handsome results from their use. But you can press into service almost anything your kitchen offers—tea cups or custard cups or individual soufflé dishes for single servings, larger soufflé dishes or mixing bowls of any size or cake pans—round, square, oblong, loaf, tube—or casseroles for whole-company service. Just make certain you don't use a pan with a removable bottom, such as a flan pan or a springform, or you're likely to have leakage problems.

There's little to do to prepare a mold or its substitute. Simply rinse it in cold water, and shake out the water—don't dry it. Or oil it, very lightly and evenly, with vegetable oil, spreading the oil on with a pad of paper towel. Or, if you like, you can use one of the commercial pan sprays—again, apply it lightly and evenly.

If the mixture you are putting into the mold is liquid, simply pour it in, and by one of the useful laws of physics the liquid wll fill every convolution of the mold, no matter how intricate. But if the mixture is partially set, or if it is made up of varying textures—a meat or fish or poultry salad, perhaps, with cubes of meat, chopped vegetables, snips of herb, plus the medium that contains the gelatin—spoon the mixture in carefully, gently pushing and packing a little at a time so that every nook and cranny is completely filled. If you don't take pains, the salad, when it is turned out, will have unsightly holes in it to spoil the effect.

To decorate a molded salad, follow the instructions for aspics (see Index), using aspic from the recipes there as a medium in which to set decorations for savory salads. Or use a little of the clear gelatin mixture—before any other ingredient is added—for any kind of salad, following the recipe you are using. For example, in making a fish or seafood salad, the basic gelatin mixture is often lemon-flavored—use that gelatin before the fish, chopped celery or cucumber, mayonnaise and any other ingredients that go into the salad are added. Spoon a little of it into the mold, let it set, add decorations and let them set, then add the finished salad mixture, spooning it in carefully so that it does not disturb the garnish but does fill all the convolutions of the mold.

What to use as a garnish? For meat salads, vegetable shapes (see Index) or sprigs of parsley or watercress, or shredded vegetables—any of the garnishes suggested for pâtés. Or strips of the meat used in the salad in combination with cheese strips, or bits of vegetable. For fish or seafood salads, sprigs of dill, cucumber slices or shapes cut with canapé cutters from cucumber peel, or halves or quarters of lemon slices or, again, vegetable shapes of almost any kind. Almost anything that springs to your mind or comes to your hand will serve well as a garnish, provided that it is edible and that its flavor is compatible with that of the main ingredient of the salad.

Extremely intricate molds seldom need a garnish set in them, but they do profit from being surrounded by greens, and/or by something—deviled eggs, for instance—that adds to the substance of the salad. Or you can surround such a salad with a variation on the main ingredient—crab legs around a crab salad, for example. Or use any of the cut fruit or vegetable garnishes suggested in this and other sections of the book to dress the plate on which the salad is unmolded.

Ring molds, large or individual, are particularly useful because they offer the opportunity for filling the center of the ring with something that adds to both the taste and appearance of the salad. A ring of a ham mixture might enclose a piled-high waldorf salad. A ring of fruit salad could be complemented by a mound of melon balls with sprigs of mint. A fish salad could surround marinated cucumbers with dill. Even so simple a decoration as a pretty bowl of the dressing to be served with the salad, set in the center of the ring, gives the plate a festive look.

Whatever salad you serve, on whatever occasion, you'll be proud of your creation if you take the necessary few minutes required to dress it with an appropriate garnish.

Garnishing Vegetables

When vegetables are used as a border around the main dish, they become an excellent garnish in themselves. But when they arrive at the table alone in a serving dish, they need a bit of dressing up—usually the addition of something that not only makes them look better, but taste better as well. Children know a fact that the rest of us try not to face: vegetables can be dull. Good for you, but on the blah side. It's the garnish that takes them out of that class for youngsters and adults alike.

There is, however, no point in garnishing a vegetable that has lived and suffered too long. Old, tired vegetables are a waste of time and money. Young, tender fresh vegetables, or well-packaged frozen ones, are still a waste of time and money if they are overcooked, so that they come to the table limp and tasteless and mud-colored.

The starting point for a vegetable that is welcomed is the cooking pot. If you have the oven on for some other purpose, baking vegetables (covered, without water, with butter if you wish and any other seasonings you like) is a great idea. They'll take longer than they would on top of the stove, but you'll be rewarded with better looks and better flavor. If you cook on top of the stove, follow two precepts: be parsimonious with the water and brief with the cooking time. A good, heavy pan with a well-fitting lid can cook vegetables in a short time in virtually no water. (Nor does it always have to be water—either broth or bouillon makes a fine vegetable-cookery medium.) Or pan the vegetables in a heavy, covered skillet that gives them plenty of room; use butter or margarine, a small amount of liquid, and seasonings as you wish. Using this method, cooking is even briefer. Coarsely shredded cabbage, sliced zucchini, and summer squash are three of the many vegetables that take kindly to panning. Spinach, to be at its best, needs only wilting in the water that clings to its leaves after washing. Other greens need a little longer—but not necessarily forever, with a ham hock, for heaven's sake!

For most vegetables, tender-crisp is the watchword. If your mother was one of those otherwise exemplary ladies who cooked vegetables until they screamed for mercy, you may find that the tender-crisp idea takes a bit of getting used to. But once over that hurdle, you'll love it. You'll realize you never really tasted vegetables before.

The butter route

Sometimes just a chunk of butter, melting as the hot dish with its hot contents is hurried from kitchen to table, is all that is needed to dress a vegetable. Or a chunk of butter plus a sprinkle of white pepper or a grinding of black.

Sometimes the butter needs to be melted in advance, so that some savory something may be added to it—lemon juice to dress asparagus, for example. Often the butter can stay in the pan until it is browned, to provide both color and flavor in dressing a dead-white vegetable, such as cauliflower. Browned butter is fine on potatoes, too. Keep an eye on it— browned butter can quickly become burned butter if you aren't vigilant. Even though the French say beurre noir, they don't really mean black. Better beurre noisette, a lively nut-brown color, with a nutty flavor.

With certain vegetables, delightful results are obtained by combining the cooking liquid with melted butter. To the melted butter (browned or not) add a little flour, along with salt and some white pepper. Stir in the liquid in which the vegetable was cooked, bring the sauce to a boil, and pour it over the vegetable. This dresses and seasons carrots, wax beans, and beets, to name just three. For extra embellishment, sprinkle the carrots with chopped mint, the beans with chopped watercress, and the beets with grated or slivered orange peel. Try this trick with other vegetables, too—it retains the vitamins leached out into the cooking water and lends the dish a touch of style.

The pork–vegetable affinity

Despite the sour comment on greens cooked forever with a ham hock, it's true that the flavors of pork and vegetables go well together. If you have a few remnants of leftover ham, sliver them to garnish green or wax beans, cauliflower, broccoli, cabbage, brussels sprouts, yams or sweet potatoes, or any greens. Bacon left over from breakfast or newly fried and crumbled can go the same route. If there's no leftover bacon, warm the leftover drippings and use them to "butter" the dinner vegetable. Thin slices of little pork sausages, either leftover or freshly cooked, dress vegetables tastily, too. Or dice salt pork, fry it slowly until it is golden and crisp, and sprinkle it over any vegetable you like. With the help of a little grated cheese, you can use these tasty pork cubes to turn chubby baked potatoes from a side dish to a main dish. Or dress braised leeks or scallions with these crunchy little salt pork pieces.

Crumbs and croutons

Fresh bread crumbs, browned to a rich golden color in butter, make a delightfully crisp dress-up for almost any vegetable. Or scatter croutons—plain, cheesed, or herbed—homemade or from a package, over the vegetable dish just before you take it to the table. Croustades (see Index) make excellent cases in which to serve creamed vegetables—they add flavor and texture and they serve to extend the vegetable, as well.

Sautéed bread—in squares or triangles or in shapes cut with a cookie cutter—is delicious with almost any vegetable. Try the following on the most confirmed spinach hater and notice the quick conversion.
Spinach superb: Thaw frozen chopped spinach in the refrigerator—count on two servings from each package. When the spinach is almost completely thawed, place it in a heavy skillet; do not add water. Cover the spinach and cook it over very low heat until it is almost dry. Season it to taste with salt, pepper, and onion powder. Add heavy cream by the spoonful, stirring and continuing to cook the spinach until the cream thickens a little. Use only enough cream to hold the spinach together. Heap the spinach in a serving dish and surround it with sautéed bread shapes, at least one for each diner.

Nuts and other crunchy toppers

Green beans amandine are by no means the be-all and end-all of vegetables-with-nuts combinations. Cashews and carrots are good partners. Pecans go well with yams, sweet potatoes, or any kind of winter squash. Peanuts are a just-right complement for celery, broccoli, beets, cabbage, and onions. Brazil nuts add a note of elegance to artichokes and asparagus.

Pinenuts and tomatoes have an affinity for one another; pinenuts are also delicious with eggplant and with artichokes. Filberts make cauliflower or peas or spinach seem very special. Water chestnuts, sliced or slivered, go well with almost anything. And don't overlook the traditional holiday combination of brussels sprouts and chestnuts.

To use nuts to dress any vegetable or vegetable combination, melt a pat of butter, add the nuts, stir them until they are heated (brown the butter and the nuts or not, as you choose), and pour them over the vegetable. Or cream the vegetable and sprinkle the nuts over the creamed dish. Consult a good general cookbook for any number of vegetable–nut recipes.

The same sort of crunch, and some very interesting flavors, can be obtained by sprinkling vegetables just before serving with toasted seeds (see Index) or with crumbled corn chips, potato chips, or matchstick potatoes from a can or package. Pretzels, too, make a tasty topper for vegetables. So do chinese noodles.

Onions everywhere

Onions go with almost anything, and they'll serve to garnish almost anything as well. Thin slivers of scallion—always remember to include some of the green tops—add looks and flavor to cauliflower, to mashed potatoes or turnips, and to almost any creamed vegetable. Or use see-through thin slices of red onion, neatly separated into rings. Rings of sweet bermuda onion do equally well on highly flavored, highly colored vegetables, such as beets and carrots. Snipped chives are enjoyed even by those who object to stronger onion flavors. Chives, too, dress up creamed vegetables. Or try them strewn liberally on braised cucumbers or zucchini or yellow or pattypan squash.

As for canned french-fried onions, they're a pantry shelf staple. Actually, they're not all that great as a substitute for homemade french-fried onions—that is, to use as a straight vegetable, with steaks or chops. But as a topper for vegetables (and for casseroles, salads, and virtually anything that needs topping, other than something sweet), they have no peer. Heat them in the oven, and crumble them or leave them as they come from the can.

Herbs, the fresh ones

In summer, when fresh herbs come up in the garden—or turn up at the greengrocer's—you can have an orgy of garnishing vegetables with them and produce some of the best flavor combinations nature has to offer. Wash and dry the herb, and snip the leaves with your kitchen scissors. Let your taste buds guide you, but here are some combinations to get you started: mint with whole baby carrots or young peas, basil with tomatoes or wax beans, summer savory with little beets or new cabbage, rosemary with summer squash or in fresh-tomato soup, dill with cucumbers (raw or cooked) or broccoli, tarragon with tender lima beans or green beans.

To make any of the fresh young vegetables into a very special dish, make an herbed green sauce. Sauce Vert, Salsa Verde—call it what you like, but spoon it over almost any vegetable your mind turns to. Here are two versions.

Green sauce: Into dairy sour cream, stir finely snipped spinach and watercress leaves and parsley and basil in whatever proportions suit your taste, but add enough so that the finished product is richly green. Season the sauce with salt and white pepper and, if you would like it a bit more tart, a little white vinegar.

Green mayonnaise: In the small bowl of an electric mixer, at medium speed, beat 2 egg yolks for 4 minutes. Combine ½ teaspoon of dry mustard, ½ teaspoon of salt, and ⅛ teaspoon of cayenne pepper; add the mixed seasonings to the yolks. Measure 1 cup of salad oil; add the oil drop by drop to the yolk mixture, beating continuously until the mixture begins to thicken. Beat in 3 tablespoons of lemon juice. Add the remaining oil in a thin stream, continuing to beat. Stop here, and you have produced a lovely, light lemony mayonnaise. Or stir in a combination of ½ cup snipped watercress leaves, ¼ cup snipped spinach leaves, and 2 tablespoons snipped tarragon leaves, and you have produced a heavenly green mayonnaise.

Broadening your horizons

There are, of course, many other sauces that beautify the appearance and enhance the taste of vegetables, whether or not they are garden fresh. Try dressing cold cooked eggplant with mayonnaise, made as above but substituting olive oil for the salad oil and wine vinegar for the lemon juice. Drench a whole cooked head of cauliflower with a nippy cheddar cheese sauce, then sprinkle it with buttered bread crumbs. (Whatever you choose to garnish cauliflower, the vegetable itself looks much more interesting if you cook the head whole, rather than breaking it up.) Another time, omit the cheese sauce and garnish the whole cauliflower with a combination of sliced scallions, finely chopped green pepper, chopped pimiento, and bread crumbs—all sautéed in butter; this is the classic Cauliflower Polonaise.

Cheese sauce, of course, does not always have to be cheddar. Swiss makes a milder sauce with a delightfully nutty flavor. Blue cheese or roquefort lends character. Every part of the country has a favorite cheese —jack, longhorn, brick, muenster, whatever—that will happily lend itself to a favorite cheese sauce.

Sometimes a plain cream sauce is just right—make it with the liquid in which the vegetables were cooked (reduced or boiled down) substituting for part of the milk or cream. Sometimes cream sauce needs a little something extra to give it panache—a tablespoon or two of lemon juice, a two-inch-long squeeze of anchovy paste, a couple of tablespoons of drained india relish, a little onion juice, some cheery red pimiento bits. Hard-cooked eggs in cream sauce are a traditional garnish for spinach, but no law says that combination won't work well on other greens or, indeed, on any reasonably strong-flavored vegetable, such as broccoli. For greater eye appeal, put the chopped whites only into the sauce, pour the sauce on the vegetable, and sieve the yolks over all.

A sweet–sour tomato sauce is very good on eggplant, zucchini, cauliflower, broccoli, or boiled onions. A bacony sweet–sour Pennsylvania Dutch dressing is great on leaf lettuce, on cooked or uncooked cabbage, and on cooked broccoli or cauliflower. It's wonderful on fried green tomatoes, too.

AMISH DRESSING   1 quart

1 teaspoon salt	2 eggs
2 tablespoons dry mustard	2 cups milk
¾ cup sugar	1 cup cider vinegar
4 tablespoons all-purpose flour	6 strips bacon
1 teaspoon onion powder	

In a heavy saucepan, combine salt, mustard, sugar, flour, and onion powder. Add eggs; mix well. Stir in milk and vinegar. Cook, stirring, over medium heat until thickened. While dressing cooks, fry bacon until crisp. Remove bacon and drain on paper towels. Remove all but 2 tablespoons of bacon drippings from pan. Into drippings, stir 1 cup of the thickened dressing. Serve hot over desired vegetable; garnish with bacon, in strips or crumbled. Cool and refrigerate remaining dressing to be used, hot or cold, at another time. Cold, without bacon, this dressing is the making of a very superior old-fashioned potato salad, with lots of scallions, garden fresh cucumbers, and hard-cooked eggs. It makes a fine farm-style coleslaw, too.

On hot broccoli, asparagus, spinach, or green beans, nothing is quite so good or so pretty as hollandaise sauce. Since the blender was invented, hollandaise has become a cinch instead of a mystery.

BLENDER HOLLANDAISE   about ⅔ cup

½ cup butter or margarine	⅛ teaspoon salt
3 egg yolks	Few grains cayenne pepper
2 tablespoons lemon juice	

Place butter in a small, heavy pan over low heat. Place egg yolk, lemon juice, salt, and cayenne in container of blender; turn blender on, then off again at once, to blend egg yolks and seasonings. When butter is melted and bubbling hot, turn blender to high speed and add butter to yolk mixture in a thin, steady stream. Turn blender off immediately when all butter is added. Serve at once, or keep warm over hot water.

Hollandaise is the sauce for classic Eggs Benedict; to make a less classic but thoroughly satisfying version to serve as an all-in-one dish for lunch or brunch, layer asparagus, broccoli, or spinach between the ham and the egg on a toasted english muffin half and top with hollandaise.

Sauce rémoulade is the right garnish for julienne strips of celery or of celery root, briefly cooked. These are generally served cold, but there certainly is no prohibition against serving them hot, if you prefer, nor is there any reason not to use this good sauce for any other purpose that its flavor suggests to you.

Sauce rémoulade: To 2 cups of mayonnaise add ½ cup of drained and finely chopped sour pickles, 2 tablespoons of drained and finely chopped capers, 1 tablespoon of dijon-style mustard, and 1 tablespoon of a combination of chopped parsley, tarragon, and chervil—let your taste guide the proportions here.

Mayonnaise, cold for contrast with a hot vegetable, or gently heated —and, sometimes, with chopped capers, pimiento, or dill pickle stirred into it—makes a good and eye-appealing vegetable sauce. For one of the world's great simple flavor combinations, try aïoli, a special, garlicky relative of mayonnaise, on cooked cabbage wedges or brussels sprouts or, most particularly, on piping hot little red-skinned new potatoes.

SAUCE AIOLI
about 1⅓ cups

6 to 8 cloves garlic (to taste)	1 cup olive oil
¼ teaspoon salt	2 tablespoons lemon juice or more
2 egg yolks	(to taste)

Crush garlic thoroughly (in a mortar, if you have one, or with the back of a spoon); add salt and crush again. Place in the small bowl of an electric mixer. Add egg yolks and mix well. Turn mixer to high speed and add a few drops of olive oil; continue adding oil, a drop or two at a time, until about 2 tablespoons have been added. Then increase to a thin stream and continue to beat until all the oil has been added. Beat in lemon juice.

Fresh from the dairy

Whatever the dairy (or the dairy case at the supermarket) has to offer can be used to make vegetables better tasting and looking. Plain cream, light or heavy, instead of butter, adds a nice touch to almost any vegetable— along with salt and freshly ground pepper. So does dairy sour cream. So does plain yogurt. Sieved lowfat cottage cheese stands in for sour cream on the vegetables of waistline watchers. But don't be heavy-handed with any of these. A judicious sprinkling of snipped chives or parsley on top contributes an additional bit of color and flavor.

Cheese of any sort, grated or shredded, dresses vegetables quickly, prettily, and deliciously. Crumble farmer cheese over delicate vegetables. Try the sharp flavor and unusual texture of feta on eggplant or on highly flavored greens such as dandelion, mustard, turnip, and kale (a few slices of greek-type olives won't go amiss here, either). Sprinkle shredded cheddar or brick thickly on almost any vegetable, run under the broiler for a few seconds for a superb cheesy, chewy crust. Chunks of fresh mozzarella are a wonderful surprise topper for ratatouille—add a dish of salty olives, another of oil-packed sardines, a loaf of crusty bread, and surprise even yourself with a great main dish for vegetable lovers.

One plus one equals one superb dish

Some vegetables have a particular affinity for one another that contributes to both the flavor and the appearance of the dish. Could middle-American cooking have gotten where it is today without the combination of carrots and peas? However—and fortunately, for variety's sake—there are other just-as-good, maybe-better, vegetable-plus-vegetable partners. Peas may be fond of carrots, but they're also good friends of green beans. Peas and wax beans are delicious, too, and make a lovely color pattern. Both peas and beans are delicious (separately, this time) when combined with mushrooms. Peas and little onions, creamed together, are a midwestern Thanksgiving tradition equally good the rest of the year. And when little new potatoes are dug in the spring, creamed potatoes and peas are a treat not to be missed.

Onions pair well with the early squashes—cucumberlike zucchini and crookneck yellow. Tomatoes and onions go well together, too. Corn and beans—green beans or lima, depending on what part of the country you're from—combine for truly American succotash. Bright diced sweet green and red peppers polka dot corn shaved from the cob for a south-of-the-border vegetable dish. Sweet white corn—shoepeg or country gentleman—is at its best paired with fresh tomatoes. Potatoes and rutabagas, half and half, mashed and running with butter—a standby during long winters when there were few fresh vegetables—is a dish that bears repeating even in these days of year-round plenty.

Almost any vegetable good singly is even better with a partner. Cook each separately, so one won't be overdone or underdone, combine them and garnish them—with butter, with crumbled bacon and a little of the bacon drippings, with slivered ham or slivered cheese, with chopped nuts, or with whatever you fancy—just before serving.

The sweet touch

Some vegetables need a touch of sweetness to bring out the best in them. Both carrots and parsnips, cut in strips and somewhat underdone, finish their cooking in a skillet with butter and a little sugar to acquire a lovely flavor and a handsome shiny glaze.

The winter squashes—hubbard, banana, butternut, acorn, and their kin—all like brown sugar. (Actually, they prefer maple, but there's little of that around these days, and what there is ought to be in Fort Knox, considering the price.) Split and seed the squash; place them face down in a pan to which you've added a little hot water. Bake them in a 375°F. oven. (Squash can be cooked at almost any temperature—so bake them at the same time as you bake your main dish.) When they are almost done, turn them over and fill their hollows with blobs of butter and spoonfuls of brown sugar. Salt them well, and return them to the oven. Or let them cook completely, scoop out and mash their pulp with butter, brown sugar, salt, and pepper. They are very good and very good looking.

If you consider sugar as a seasoning rather than as an ingredient, many vegetables profit from the judicious use of it. Children cry for marshmallows on their already-candied yams or sweet potatoes. We all know the virtue of molasses in baked beans. A little sugar in the water in which rather elderly peas are cooked gives them a second childhood. The liquid for cooking corn should be sugared, never salted (and that liquid should be equal parts of milk and water). Virtually any tomato dish—and this includes even spaghetti sauce—is the better for a little sugar added with the other seasonings. It diminishes the sometimes too-acid taste. But go easy. Better to taste and add a bit more sugar if necessary than to taste and think, "I'll have to serve it for dessert!"

Getting it all together

Good food, well cooked and well seasoned, is one of life's simple but great pleasures. Well cooked, well seasoned, *and* well garnished, food is a delight to the eye and the palate, a garnerer of compliments, a pleaser of family and guests, a source of pardonable pride for the cook. There is for her in the preparing and the serving a knowledge of accomplishment, a sense of satisfaction very good for her self-esteem.

Sweet Decorations

Desserts made at home and decorated at home, presented with a becoming combination of modesty and pride, are a demonstration of the pleasure you take in preparing food that is lovely to look at and delightful to eat, that is a compliment to family and guests.

Decorations for such desserts can be very simple or ambitiously complicated, depending on your skill and your taste. First and foremost, though, the food that is the reason for the decoration must be good—made from a trustworthy recipe that you have carefully followed, using high-quality ingredients. The most elaborate decoration in the world won't disguise a so-so dessert—in fact, all that frou-frou will only point up the food's basic mediocrity.

There is a bakery in New York City that prides itself on its elaborately decorated productions—handsome, mile-high cakes, ingeniously frosted; petits fours covered with unblemished icing, ornamented with crystallized violets; pies whose crusts and elaborately conceived borders shine with dorure; tarts with each piece of fruit set separately in its place, gleamingly glazed. The store itself is very attractive and looks to be scrupulously clean. Yet when you enter, you are greeted not with the incomparable aroma of baking, but with an off-putting odor that results from the smell of slightly rancid oil combined with that of imitation vanilla extract. And the goodies, when you bite into them, give you nothing—virtually no flavor, texture like plastic foam, icings resistant enough to break a tooth on. All these things are incredibly expensive—and people must buy them, for the place has been in business for a long time.

Another bakery, two blocks away, smells right, and its products taste right. But whoever in that kitchen does the decorating must be a color-blind megalomaniac, a disorder that reaches its apogee in his cakes for special occasions. Tier on tier they rise, loaded with swags and borders and bands and stripes of decorator's icing in a mesmerizing rainbow of colors, each fighting for supremacy. Tender messages on their tops are worked out in decorator's gel in some color antagonistic to the frosting on which they sit. The whole is crowned with a cascade of roses. Plastic roses. More often than not, *blue* plastic roses.

Without a doubt, you get the point: simplicity and restraint should be the watchwords in decorating cakes or any other desserts to prevent ornamentation from becoming vulgarity, vulgarity progressing to the point of obscenity. Getting loose in the kitchen with all that color, all those ideas, all those tools, can be a heady experience. Control yourself!

Cakes for All-Thumbs Decorators

Even if you are one of those good cooks who is cursed with two left hands —and they do occur occasionally—you can still produce a cake with appearance to match its fine shape, flavor, and texture. A beautiful cake does not have to be decorated through the use of special frostings, pastry bags, tubes, tips, and the like. All you need is a little know-how (supplied here), plus a little good taste (yours), plus a few simple supermarket-bought items and your own kitchen tools.

Whether or not you are skillful with your hands, there are times when an elaborately decorated, looks-as-if-it-came-from-the-caterer cake is out of place. At those times you'll want to produce a pretty, well-dressed—but not overdressed—cake suited to the occasion. Just be sure, no matter how you intend to ornament it, that first of all it's a *good* cake. With that, you're much more than halfway home.

A few basics

It's been said that in order to be a good cook, all you need is to know how to read. Up to a point, that's true. If you can read a recipe and follow its instructions to the letter, you'll make a good cake—provided that it's a good recipe. When you're making a cake that you want to be impressive, don't choose a recipe whose title is synonymous with "economical." If the recipe is called something like Grandma's Eggless, Butterless, Milkless Special, pass it by. Maybe it's good, but what it would be good for is dessert on a night when you're in a hurry or for the children's lunches, not for a special occasion.

Don't make a cake for guests from a recipe you've never used before. Try it on the family first, unless you're an exceptional cook who can tell simply by reading the recipe that the results will be good. Be sure, by checking the recipe in advance, that you have all the ingredients on hand. Make certain, too, that you have a pan of the size the recipe calls for. In a great many areas of cooking, substitutions or makeshifts can be employed in a fairly cavalier manner, but cake baking is not one of them. Use the pan called for or one of the proper alternates from the table below.

Be certain, too, that your oven thermostat is properly calibrated. The utility that supplies the fuel to run your oven—the local gas and/or electric company—will check the accuracy of your oven thermostat as a customer service. Have it done. It pays. A too-hot oven will make the cake rise too fast, cause an unsightly bump on top and, perhaps, holes inside. If the oven is too cool, the cake may not rise at all, or at least not to its proper capacity, and the result will be heavy and soggy.

Useful bits of know-how

Use, we admonished you, the size cake pan called for in the recipe. However, with the following list to guide you, you can make certain substitutions if your plan of decorating or serving calls for a different shape.

a recipe that yields:	can also be baked as:
two 8-inch layers	two thin 8-inch squares *or* eighteen to twenty-four 2½-inch cupcakes
three 8-inch layers	two 9-inch squares
two 9-inch layers	two 8-inch squares *or* three thin 8-inch layers *or* one 15- × 10- × 1-inch rectangle *or* thirty 2½-inch cupcakes
one 8- × 8- × 2-inch square	one 9-inch layer
two 8- × 8- × 2-inch squares	two 9-inch layers *or* one 13- × 9- × 2-inch rectangle
one 9- × 9- × 2-inch square	two thin 8-inch layers
two 9- × 9- × 2-inch squares	three 8-inch layers
one 13- × 9- × 2-inch rectangle	two 9-inch layers *or* two 8- × 8- × 2-inch squares
one 9- × 5- × 3-inch loaf cake	one 9- × 9- × 2-inch square *or* twenty-four to thirty 2½-inch cupcakes
one 8- × 4- × 3-inch loaf cake	one 8- × 8- × 2-inch square
one 9- × 3½-inch tube cake	two 9-inch layers *or* twenty-four to thirty 2½-inch cupcakes
one 10- × 4-inch tube cake	two 9- × 5- × 3-inch loaves *or* one 13- × 9- × 2-inch rectangle

If you are baking a single panful of cake batter, place the oven rack in the center of the oven, the cake pan on the center of the rack. If you're going to bake more than one pan of batter at a time, a bit of strategy is called for. Two pans can generally be accommodated on the one center-of-the-oven rack. Three pans require two racks, occupying the center third of the oven. Place one pan at the left of the upper rack, toward the back; the second pan at the right of the upper rack, toward the front; and the third pan on the bottom rack, slightly left of center. Hopscotch four pans so that neither of the pans on the lower rack is directly under either of the pans on the upper rack.

In any case, no two pans should touch one another, nor should any pan touch the walls of the oven. If your oven is small, or if you have any doubts, don't bake more than two pans of batter at once. Cakes that are too crowded rise unevenly, are difficult to frost, and never look the way you had pictured them, no matter how carefully you put them together, how lavish you are with frosting and/or decorations.

Sometimes you may wish to cut a tall cake that has been baked in a springform or tube pan into layers or to split a cake layer into two equal layers. There's a neat and easy way. Mark the cake all the way around or on all sides with food picks. (If your eye is good, fine; if you're not sure of yourself, use a ruler to measure. Little mistakes made along the way have a nasty habit of magnifying themselves in the finished product.) Using a sawtooth knife, cut through the cake, using the picks as a guide. Or, with the picks to guide you, pull heavy sewing thread back and forth through the cake with a gentle sawing motion.

Working toward a grand conclusion

Some home economists and/or professional cake decorators pride themselves on being able to frost cakes with, so to speak, their bare hands. They balance the cake on the palm of their left hand while (using a spatula) slathering the frosting on with their right, sometimes waltzing about the kitchen as they work. This is sheer exhibitionism and often results, even among these experts, in sending out to the bakery for a cake and giving the kitchen floor a mopping it would not otherwise have needed.

Set the cake to be frosted on a plate—a flat one without a rim—that is at least 2 inches larger in circumference. Or use a cake stand or, if you do this often or plan to, get a revolving cake stand with a top that turns as you frost. Just be certain that the plate on which you frost the cake is the one on which you are going to serve it—transferring a big frosted cake from one plate to another is an invitation to disaster. And don't feel called upon to put a doily—paper or linen—between cake and plate. This is one of those nasty-nice affectations left over from the Victorians. Doilies always get rucked up and soiled when the cake is cut, and the whole effect is sloppy.

If you're going to frost the cake on the plate on which it will be served, how do you keep from slobbering frosting all over the plate? Easy. Tear off four pieces of waxed paper, each the width of the roll and 3 inches deep. Arrange them so that they form a hollow square on the cake plate and overhang the edge a trifle. Put the cake in place and frost it. Then, tugging gently, remove the waxed paper.

For optimum good looks, frost tube cakes and cakes baked in bundt pans upside down—that is, what was the bottom of the cake while it was in the pan becomes the top when you frost it. Flat, single-layer cakes are frosted topside up. When frosting layer cakes, place the first layer bottomside up and spread it with frosting or filling to within ¼ inch of the edge. Put the second layer on the filling bottomside down.

Before you begin to frost, brush away any loose crumbs. If there is an unsightly bulge on top of the cake, slice it off. Then spread the whole cake with a very thin layer of frosting and let it stand for 10 minutes to set. This preliminary frosting will trap crumbs and form a base for the remaining frosting. Frost the sides of the cake first and then the top, spreading the frosting out to meet at the edges.

In the usual course of things, you can cut a round cake in wedges and make a square or rectangular cake in squares or rectangles of any size that suits you. However, there are times when a preplanned cutting pattern should be worked out—particularly when a big cake and a large number of guests are involved, more particularly when a cake of any size must yield more servings than you had in mind when you made it.

To cut a butter cake: Use a thin-pointed, sharp knife, cutting with a sawing motion. Wipe off the blade after each cut.

To cut a foam cake (chiffon, angel food, sponge): Use a cake breaker —a special tool with a series of long teeth—or pull pieces apart gently with two forks, holding one in each hand.

To cut a rolled cake (jelly roll, chocolate cream roll): Use a piece of heavy white sewing thread about 15 inches long; slip it under the roll at the point where you want to cut, bring up the ends and cross them over the top, one in each hand; pull the ends down, in opposite directions, to cut a slice.

To store a cake: Keep a frosted cake in a cake keeper—a flat surface of glass, ceramic, or plastic with a high, domed cover that fits snugly enough to prevent the cake from drying out. Or invert a big bowl or cooking pot over the cake. An unfrosted cake can be wrapped in foil or plastic wrap. All cakes, with the exception of those frosted or filled with whipped cream or those that have a cream or custard filling, can be stored at room temperature. Most cakes can be frozen—preferably unfrosted.

Getting down to—or up to—decorating your cake

Plan to make the cake you're going to serve guests well in advance—the day before, or certainly early in the morning of the day you'll serve it. That way, you won't feel pushed. Remember, too, that cakes take time to make, time to bake, time to cool, time to frost and decorate, and time for the frosting and/or decoration to set after it's been applied. That all adds up. Anyway, unless it's a "come for dessert and coffee" party—a very pleasant way to entertain—you'll have other things to do, other parts of the meal to prepare. Get the cake out of the way early.

Whether for family or for guests, planned and prepared well in advance or whipped up at the last minute, any cake that is worth making is worth frosting or, at the very least, topping in some manner that will add to the looks and the flavor of the finished product. Except for some pound cakes and some fruit cakes, an undressed cake sits mournfully on its plate looking as if nobody cared. Even pound cakes and fruit cakes are the better for a little dressing up.

There are canned frostings and packaged frosting mixes available to the totally timid, and some of these products are, if not glorious, adequate. However, if you've had the gumption to make a cake, you might as well make a topping or frosting for it.

No-frosting cake toppers

Here are a few of the possible ways to avoid frosting a cake and still have it come to the table looking finished and tasting good. Some of these are homey, some relatively gala, but all are both tasty and pretty.

Broiled topper: To cheer up a simple 8-inch-square cake, combine 1/3 cup of soft butter or margarine, 2/3 cup of firmly packed brown sugar, 1/4 cup of heavy cream, 1/2 teaspoon of vanilla extract, 1/3 cup of chopped pecans (or walnuts), and 2/3 cup of flaked coconut. Spread the mixture evenly over a warm cake. Place it under the broiler, about 6 inches away from the source of heat, and broil it until the topping is bubbly and beginning to brown, about 3 minutes. Keep your eye on it—it scorches very easily.

The doily ploy: Doilies, it was pointed out, are a nuisance under a cake. But on top of it—ah, that's something else. Center a paper doily on the top of a flat-surfaced cake, positioning it neatly so that the pattern is even all around. Place confectioners sugar in a small-mesh sieve (a tea strainer is fine) and sprinkle it over the top of the doily. Be generous with the sugar. Remove the doily carefully, lifting it straight up, and you'll leave a handsome sugar snowflake on the cake's surface.

If you have previously buried a vanilla bean in the sugar to flavor it, so much the better. And if you have baked your cake in a bundt pan or a turk's head or some other decorative mold, simply sprinkle the top with confectioners sugar, without benefit of doily.

The chocolate mint way: As soon as a cake is out of the oven, place chocolate-covered mint patties on the hot surface. Give them a few moments to melt and then swirl them over the cake in a marblelike pattern of chocolate and creamy filling.

The chocolate bits way: As soon as the cake is done, sprinkle the hot surface generously with semisweet chocolate bits. Return the cake to the oven briefly—the bits will soften but not melt entirely. Then remove the cake from the oven and sprinkle the chocolate surface with chopped pecans, walnuts, or pistachios. Stop there, or add a few miniature marshmallows for a rocky road topping to delight children—and adults.

If you'd like to make a festive but unfrosted cake for a company-coming occasion, here's one that will please both you and the guests.

Frozen party cake: Make, bake, and cool two 9-inch cake layers, either vanilla or chocolate. Split each layer through the center to make two layers. Into each of three foil-lined 9-inch layer cake pans, spread 1 pint of softened ice cream—all one flavor, or any assortment that you like. Strawberry ice cream with a vanilla cake is a pretty combination; pistachio ice cream with a chocolate cake makes a delightful contrast of flavors and colors. Freeze the ice cream until it is very firm; then remove it from the pans, peel off the foil, and put the cake layers together with the ice cream layers between. Freeze the whole concoction until serving time. Cut the cake in wedges and pass hot chocolate sauce or a sauce of crushed and sweetened fruit to drizzle over it.

A good homemade sauce on a good homemade plain cake makes a superb dessert. Bake a cake of whatever flavor you wish in a square or rectangular pan. Serve it warm or cooled, with any one of these delicious sauces, all of which can be made in advance and reheated, if desired, or served cold. Any good general cookbook will supply you with recipes for a dozen more sauces to use in the same way.

BITTERSWEET MOCHA SAUCE
about 1½ cups

2 teaspoons instant coffee powder
3 (1-ounce) squares unsweetened
   chocolate
¼ cup heavy cream

1 cup sugar
1 tablespoon butter or margarine
½ teaspoon vanilla extract

In a saucepan, dissolve coffee powder in ½ cup boiling water. Add chocolate and cream and cook over low heat, stirring constantly, until chocolate is melted and mixture is smooth. Add sugar and butter; cook over moderate heat, stirring constantly, until sugar is dissolved; continue to cook until mixture is slightly thickened, 4 to 5 minutes. Blend in vanilla. Cover and refrigerate until ready to serve. Serve at room temperature or slightly warmed.

CHOCOLATE RUM SAUCE
about 1¼ cups

3 (1-ounce) squares unsweetened
   chocolate, broken up
2 teaspoons instant coffee powder
¼ cup milk
⅔ cup sugar

1 tablespoon butter or margarine
Few grains salt
½ teaspoon vanilla extract
3 tablespoons rum (or to taste)

Place chocolate in a saucepan; add coffee powder, milk, and ½ cup water. Cook over low heat, stirring constantly, until smooth. Add sugar, butter, and salt; cook over moderate heat, stirring constantly, until slightly thickened, 3 to 5 minutes. Remove from heat; blend in vanilla and rum. Cover and refrigerate until ready to serve. Serve chilled or heated.

MINTED PINEAPPLE SAUCE
about 2½ cups

1 (13¼-ounce) can crushed
   pineapple
1 teaspoon cornstarch

⅔ cup light corn syrup
⅔ cup mint jelly

In a saucepan, combine undrained pineapple and cornstarch. Cook over low heat, stirring constantly, until mixture boils and is clear and thickened; remove from heat. In another saucepan, cook corn syrup until it comes to a full boil; continue to cook, stirring constantly, 2 minutes. Remove from heat; add pineapple mixture and blend well. Add jelly and stir until it is melted. Cover and refrigerate until ready to serve. Serve cold or at room temperature.

CREAMY BUTTERSCOTCH SAUCE

about 1½ cups

1 cup firmly packed dark brown
  sugar
½ cup granulated sugar
⅔ cup undiluted evaporated milk

¼ teaspoon salt
¼ cup butter or margarine
2 tablespoons light corn syrup
1 teaspoon vanilla extract

In a saucepan, combine all ingredients except vanilla. Bring to a boil over low heat, stirring constantly. Continue to cook 3 minutes. Blend in vanilla. Cover and refrigerate until ready to serve. Serve at room temperature or reheated.

WHOLE STRAWBERRY SAUCE

about 2 cups

1 (16-ounce) package frozen whole
  strawberries

½ cup light corn syrup

Thaw berries; drain juice into a saucepan and add corn syrup. Bring to a boil over moderate heat and boil 5 minutes. Cool; add strawberries. Cover and refrigerate until ready to serve. Serve cold or at room temperature; do not reheat.

FLUFFY ORANGE SAUCE

about 1¾ cups

¼ cup butter or margarine
1 cup sifted confectioners sugar
1 egg, separated

¼ cup orange juice
1 teaspoon grated orange peel

Cream butter until soft. Gradually beat in confectioners sugar; continue to beat until mixture is fluffy. Beat egg yolk; stir into butter mixture with orange juice and peel. Beat egg white until stiff. Fold into butter mixture. Cover and refrigerate. Serve cold.

HEADY APRICOT SAUCE

about 3½ cups

1 (8-ounce) package dried apricots
1 cup sugar

3 tablespoons kirsch (or to taste)

Place apricots in saucepan; cover with water. Cook over moderate heat until apricots are very tender, 30 to 40 minutes. Drain apricots, reserving liquid. Measure liquid; if necessary, add water to make 2 cups. Place about ⅓ of the apricots and ¼ of the liquid in container of blender; blend on low speed until puréed. Repeat with remaining apricots and liquid. Return puréed mixture to saucepan; add sugar and cook over moderate heat, stirring, until sugar is dissolved. Blend in kirsch. Cover and refrigerate until ready to serve. Serve warm or reheated.

There are a number of good dessert sauces, in cans or jars, available on the market. Canned fruit-pie fillings, heated and judiciously flavored with rum or brandy or kirsch, also make acceptable sauces for plain

Opposite: Angel food cake with fresh flowers, lemon bundt cake with fresh lemons, mocha loaf with melted-chocolate topping

cake. Or boil maple syrup for 3 to 4 minutes to thicken it slightly and add chopped walnuts.

If you don't want to sauce it, glazing it is the next-easiest, next-quickest way to dress up a plain cake, particularly an angel food, sponge, or chiffon cake.

Orange glaze (particularly good on nut cake): Blend 1 cup of sifted confectioners sugar with 1 tablespoon of orange juice. Add more orange juice, a little at a time, until the glaze is thin enough to pour from a spoon. Spoon the mixture over the cake. If you like, decorate the glazed cake with thin slivers of orange peel and/or chopped nuts.

Chocolate glaze: Break up 1 (4-ounce) package of sweet cooking chocolate into a saucepan; add 1 tablespoon of butter and 3 tablespoons of water. Cook the glaze over moderate heat, stirring until the chocolate is melted. Remove the glaze from the heat and beat in 1 cup of sifted confectioners sugar, 1/8 teaspoon of salt, and 1 teaspoon of vanilla extract. Spread the mixture over the cake.

Raspberry glaze: Thaw and drain 1 package of frozen raspberries and press them through a sieve to purée them and remove the seeds. Stir sufficient purée into 2 cups of sifted confectioners sugar to obtain a pouring consistency. Slowly spoon the glaze over the cooled cake, letting it run down the sides.

Mocha glaze: Over hot water, melt 2 (1-ounce) squares of unsweetened chocolate with 1 teaspoon of butter. Stir in 1 cup of sifted confectioners sugar. Add 3 tablespoons of very strong cold coffee, beating the mixture until smooth. Spoon the glaze over the cake immediately.

Whipped cream, sweetened and flavored with vanilla extract, is the simplest of frostings—spread it over the top and sides of a sponge, angel food, or chiffon cake, or use it to frost and fill a layer cake. (Remember to store a cake thus frosted in the refrigerator if you're not going to serve it at once and to return any leftovers to the refrigerator.) Or try this quick and easy, tastier and dressier version on a chocolate or nut layer cake.

Chocolate cream: In a large mixer bowl, combine 1 (14-ounce) package of chocolate fudge frosting mix, 2 cups of heavy cream, and 2 teaspoons of vanilla extract. (If you like a mocha flavor, add 1 teaspoon of instant coffee powder.) Beat the mixture at medium-high speed until it is stiff, use it as both filling and frosting. Refrigerate the frosted cake until it is well chilled.

Whipped cream cheese—either the ready-whipped or regular cream cheese combined with a little milk or cream and beaten until fluffy—makes an excellent topper for spice cake or gingerbread. If you like, flavor it with a little grated lemon peel.

Getting a bit more ambitious

A homemade cake covered with homemade frosting is a pleasure to look at and to eat. It can be an even greater pleasure if you dress up the frosting a bit; the results will be so rewarding you'll be delighted that you took the few moments' extra time.

Suppose you've made a fudge or devil's food cake and crowned it with white frosting—butter cream, seven-minute, whatever—or pale golden seafoam frosting. For an extra touch, melt together 2 (1-ounce) squares of semisweet chocolate and 2 tablespoons of light corn syrup. Allow it to cool and then drizzle it around the edges of the cake, letting a little drip down the sides.

Another time, with another chocolate-flavored cake, tint the white frosting a very pale green with liquid or paste food coloring and flavor it with almond extract. After the cake is frosted, sprinkle the top with a combination of chopped pistachio nuts and grated semisweet chocolate.

A word about food coloring, which can be used to tint frosting any shade you like—to go with the flavor of the frosting or of the cake itself. Food coloring comes in two forms: liquid and paste. The liquid is available in yellow, red, blue, and green, to use as is or to combine into almost any color you wish. Paste colors, more expensive and not as widely available, come in a greater range of colors. In using either, take it easy. Add a very tiny bit of the color—a drop of the liquid, a small amount of the paste taken up on the tip of a food pick—and blend it into the frosting thoroughly. Repeat, if necessary, to get the color you want. It's easy to add more but impossible to take out color once it's been added. Pastels are pretty, but deep-colored frostings are off-putting.

Here are some more simple, easy ways to turn your frosted cake into a handsome production.

Simple crisscross: On a smooth-spread butter frosting, make parallel lines by drawing the tines of a fork through the frosting, leaving a space the width of the fork between the strokes. Give the cake a 90° turn and draw a second set of lines at right angles to the first.

Chocolate web: Melt unsweetened or semisweet chocolate and drizzle it in concentric circles on top of a round cake that has been frosted in white or a pale color. Draw the tip of a knife lightly through the chocolate from the center to the edges in as many places as you like, creating the effect of a web.

Double crisscross: On a smoothly frosted square or rectangular cake (with the frosting set until almost firm), mark the frosting into squares with the tip of a knife. Using the tines of a fork, press lines in each square, alternating their direction from square to square.

Chocolate swags: On a square or rectangular cake smoothly frosted in white or a pale color, drizzle melted chocolate in thin parallel lines about an inch apart. At right angles, draw the tip of a knife through the chocolate lines—also about an inch apart—first toward you, then away from you, to form a series of scallops.

Swirlaway: On the top of any shape cake, frosted in any flavor or color, draw parallel straight lines about 1 inch apart with the tip of a knife. Draw a second series of lines at right angles to the first. Using the tip of the knife and wiping it clean after each use, form a small swirl in the frosting in the center of each square. Or press the tip of a small spatula or an after-dinner coffee spoon into the frosting in each square, leaving a simple leaf shape—again, wiping the utensil clean after each use. Or, if the frosting is a pale color, drizzle the lines on with melted chocolate rather than drawing them on, and then make a swirl or leaf pattern in each square.

There are, of course—aren't there always—a multitude of possible variations on any or all of these. Instead of drawing a pattern in the squares or shapes created by any of these means, press a perfect half nutmeat into each square or into alternating squares to make a checkerboard pattern. Or press in a piece of candied ginger. Or half of a candied or minted cherry. Or alternate squares of the fork-tine pattern with squares containing nuts or ginger or cherries. Or press small, attractive candies into the squares. Or fill alternating squares with colored sugar or candy sprinkles or chocolate sprinkles.

Just a little something extra

You need not, of course, make a pattern on your frosting before adding a decoration. A simple row of nutmeats ringing the top edge dresses up a round cake very nicely. Or leave the icing on top of the cake unadorned, patterned only by the (neat and even, or riotously swirled) marks of the knife or spatula you used in frosting it, and press chopped nuts of any sort into the frosting around the sides of the cake. Or use whole almonds, blanched or not, to press any pattern you like into the frosting. Or use the tines of a fork to striate the sides of the cake in close-together up-and-down lines.

Nuts aren't the only possible decoration of this kind. Candies, whole or crushed, are very good—lemon drops on a lemon cake, for instance, or peppermint candy on a chocolate cake, or chocolate bits making polka dots on a pale frosting. Or go a step further and make praline, the delicious candylike concoction that professional bakers of elegant cakes like to use, or a close relative, made with black walnuts. Both are really very easy to make and they are absolutely delicious—hide them, or the family will eat up your efforts before they ever get to the cake. Crushed lightly, either of these can be used to coat a frosting all over or in a pattern; pulverized and folded into whipped cream, either makes a most elegant and luscious frosting and filling. Roll praline to a powder with a rolling pin, between two sheets of waxed paper, or pulverize it in the blender.

PRALINE

2 cups sugar	¾ cup shelled almonds
¾ cup shelled filberts	

Place sugar in a heavy skillet over low heat; cook until sugar begins to melt. Stir in filberts and almonds all at once and continue to cook, without further stirring, until the mixture turns a rich amber. Pour onto a lightly buttered baking sheet, and allow the mixture to cool and harden completely.

Crushed, this amount of praline will decorate two cakes and leave a little over for the youngsters to sample. Pulverized, it yields about 3 cups. The powder keeps well when stored in airtight containers. The praline may also be used as a flavoring—for example, use 2 tablespoons to flavor the pastry cream used to fill eclairs, or stir some into a simple custard or tapioca pudding for a wonderful, never-before taste treat.

BLACK WALNUT BRITTLE

1 cup sugar	2 tablespoons butter or margarine,
½ cup light corn syrup	softened
1 cup black walnuts, coarsely	1 teaspoon baking soda
broken	

In a heavy 2-quart saucepan, combine sugar and corn syrup; add ¼ cup water. Over medium heat, bring mixture to a boil, stirring until sugar is dissolved. Stir in black walnuts. Place candy thermometer in pan. Continue to cook, stirring frequently, until temperature reaches 300°F. (the hard-crack stage). Remove the candy from heat; immediately stir in butter and baking soda. Pour at once onto a large, buttered baking sheet. Cool.

As candy, this makes about 1 pound. (If you don't like black walnuts, you may substitute regular english walnuts or unsalted peanuts.) When it has hardened, break it into pieces with your hands. Or crush it coarsely or pulverize it for the same uses as praline, above.

Cautionary note—candy-decorated cakes are best kept refrigerated until it is time to bring them to the table. Sometimes the broken or crushed candies get very sticky at room temperature, and they may even melt in a hot kitchen.

Any flavor, as long as it's chocolate

Cakes decorated with chocolate in any of several forms—curls, cutouts, molds, or simply grated—should also be refrigerated. But if this is a drawback, it's the only one. Chocolate decorations are very handsome, and, of course, to some people there is no flavor other than chocolate, so they are welcomed for more than their good looks. They can make a nicely frosted cake into a very festive dessert indeed, fit to grace almost any occasion. In using any of these decorations, don't stint—pile chocolate curls on top of a cake or very gently press them into the frosting all around the sides. If you are using cutouts or molds, make enough so that the finished cake has a rich, lavish appearance.

Chocolate curls: With the heat of your hands or in a barely warm oven, slightly soften squares of semisweet chocolate. Using a vegetable peeler, shave the chocolate—it will accommodatingly make itself into curls.

Chocolate cutouts: In a double boiler, over hot but not boiling water, melt ¼ cup of semisweet chocolate pieces with 2 teaspoons of butter or margarine. Line a baking sheet with waxed paper. Pour the chocolate mixture onto the paper and spread it into an 8- x 6-inch rectangle. Refrigerate the chocolate until it is hard. At the same time, refrigerate a spatula and the small cookie cutters to be used in cutting the chocolate. When the chocolate is hard, cut it with the chilled cutters and transfer the cutouts to the cake with the chilled spatula. Refrigerate the cake until serving time.

Chocolate molds: The chocolate mixture above may be poured into chilled tiny molds. (These can be purchased at stores which sell candy- and cake-decorating equipment, or see Tools of the Trade.) Refrigerate the filled molds until the chocolate is hard; turn out the candy and use it to decorate the cake. Again, the whole cake should be refrigerated until serving time.

Chocolate—cool, but not so cold that it is brittle—can be shaved with a sharp knife, or grated on a kitchen grater, to use as decoration.

A delicious addition, to make the simplest cake seem extraordinary, is chocolate-coated fruit peel strips. Though they are a bit of a nuisance to make, they can be done well in advance and wait in the refrigerator until you need them.

CHOCOLATE-CANDIED ORANGE PEEL   about 2½ pounds

5 *large navel oranges*	2 *(8-ounce) packages semisweet*
1 *cup honey*	*chocolate squares (a total of*
1 *cup sugar (about)*	*16 1-ounce squares)*

Using a sharp knife, remove peel from oranges in quarters; cut quarters into ¼-inch-wide strips. Place strips in a 5-quart saucepan; cover with cold water. Bring to a full boil; drain. Repeat four times. Place drained peel in a large skillet. Add honey and ⅔ cup water. Cook slowly until all syrup is absorbed, about 1 hour. Continue to cook for 15 minutes, over very low heat; watch carefully so peel does not scorch. Drain thoroughly; cool. Roll each strip of peel in sugar; spread out on baking sheets in a single layer to dry overnight. The following day, roll again in sugar. In top of double boiler, over hot but not boiling water, melt chocolate. Holding candied peel with tongs or piercing it with a food pick, dip each piece in chocolate, draining off excess. Place pieces on a baking sheet lined with waxed paper. Cool, then refrigerate.

Use these delights to circle the top edge of an orange-glazed, orange-flavored chiffon cake, or a chocolate cake or nut cake, or almost any other kind of cake. The recipe will make enough to decorate a couple of cakes, and allow for a little nibbling on the side. For nonlovers of chocolate (somewhere there must be some) leave the candied peel undipped—it's a pretty and delicious decoration that way, too. And for a change, use the same recipe to candy, chocolate-dipped or not, the peel of three large grapefruit, or combine orange and grapefruit peel in one candying session.

Nuts for flavor, for texture

Nuts, plain or toasted or even, in some circumstances, salted, decorate a cake in a way interesting to both eye and palate. A burnt sugar cake, for example, with a caramel frosting, looks handsome and tastes fine with its top liberally covered with halved roasted peanuts. Put them in place on the cake in strips radiating from the center, so that the entire top of the cake is covered.

Other cakes call for other nut decorations. Blanched almonds, whole or slivered, plain or toasted, are very good and very pretty. Stud a cake frosting all over with almonds for a lovely look. (To blanch almonds at home, place them in boiling water for a minute or two, drain them, and slip off their skins with your fingers.) The lovely yellow-green of pistachios offers handsome contrast to any frosting, light or dark. (Pistachios can be skinned in the same way as almonds.) Brazil nuts are too often overlooked. To make handsome curls, soak the shelled nuts in boiling water for five minutes, slice them into thin curls with a sharp knife, then dry them in a low oven without browning. Pecans and walnuts lose nothing of their flavor and goodness just because they are so commonly used; chop them to sprinkle on the frosting or decorate a cake with plump, nut-brown halves. Whole filberts have a flavor affinity for chocolate. Whole nuts or halves of any kind can be dipped in melted chocolate so that they are only partially covered, then cooled and used for decoration.

Chestnuts are elegant. You can prepare them at home—a good general cookbook will tell you how—but they're really a terrible nuisance. They can be bought ready to use in cans or jars, brandied or in vanilla syrup or glacéed. If you're particularly fond of chestnuts (they're another of those love-them-or-hate-them foods), fill the layers of a vanilla cake with canned sweet chestnut purée, frost the cake with chocolate, and decorate it with glacéed chestnuts, just as they come from the jar.

Coconut is so versatile it's in a class by itself. One of the great American desserts is a white cake—its layers put together with a tart/ sweet lemon filling—frosted with a fluffy white frosting and drifted high with snowy coconut. Such a cake is as lovely to look at as it is to taste and needs no further embellishment. Neither does the popular German chocolate cake, with its brown sugar/pecan/coconut filling and topping. Neither, for that matter, do other big-production cakes, such as Lord and Lady Baltimore—they're beautiful in and of themselves, and decorating them is only lily-gilding.

Back to coconut. Use it plain, or toast it or color it and/or flavor it to make easy-but-beautiful decorations for almost any kind of cake.

Toasted coconut: Spread the coconut—shredded at home from the whole nut, if you're ambitious, or from a can or bag—on a baking sheet. Place it in a 300°F. oven and bake it, stirring occasionally, for 15 to 25 minutes, until it attains a toasty brown shade. It is particularly good on an almond-flavored cake with brown-butter icing.

Colored coconut: Place shredded or flaked coconut in a jar that has a lid and add a few drops of any food coloring you desire. Put the lid on the jar and shake it until the coconut is nicely tinted. Or put the coconut in a plastic bag and add the food coloring. Close the bag and knead and shake it until you get the color you want. Either way, be miserly with the coloring—it's a tint, not a shade, that you're seeking. Pastel coconut is fine for cakes that grace a child's birthday party or a shower luncheon. Suit the color to the flavor of the cake—pink for peppermint, green for almond, yellow for lemon, orange for orange. Blue? If you want blue coconut, go ahead, but blue just isn't a good color for food.

Coffee coconut: In a jar or bag, as described above, combine 1½ teaspoons of instant coffee powder with an equal amount of water. Add the flaked or shredded coconut and shake the jar or knead the bag until the coconut is colored. Spread the coconut on a baking sheet and bake it in a 300°F. oven for 20 minutes, stirring occasionally, until it is dry. Coffee coconut enhances the appearance and flavor of any cake with a mocha icing, or try it on a lemon cake with a coffee filling and a lemon frosting—it tastes as good as espresso with a twist of lemon peel.

Flowers, garden- or package-variety

Fresh flowers make a truly beautiful decoration for a cake, particularly a light one such as angel food or sunshine (what you make to use up all those leftover egg yolks after you've made the angel food cake), chiffon or sponge. When you're making such a cake, bear in mind that the traditional flavors—vanilla for angel food, lemon for sponge, and so on—are generally used not because other flavorings are against the rule, but because other cooks have no imagination. Grated chocolate gives authority to angel food; or use cocoa (¼ cup imparts a pleasant flavor) to replace a part of the flour. Flavor a sunshine cake with ginger or almond, or tint the batter a delicate pink and flavor it with strawberry or raspberry. Make a maple or a coffee or a spice chiffon cake, or a sponge cake heady with rum or brandy.

Heavily frosted, these cakes are overburdened. Glaze them instead, with a thin icing that complements or contrasts with their flavor. Then crown them with flowers. A tube cake has a central place in which a flower holder—a slim glass will do, a test tube is ideal—can be placed and filled with flowers. Then wreath the cake plate with green leaves and more flowers. Carnations or their relatives, garden pinks, make a spicily fragrant decoration, sweet peas a delicate one. Bachelor's buttons, nasturtiums, daisies, asters and small chrysanthemums, marigolds, roses, ranunculus, camellias, gardenias—all these and more make lovely fresh decorations, depending on their season in the garden or what the florist has to offer. Flowers represent one of the very few exceptions to the rule that what garnishes or decorates should also be edible.

If you want to have your flowers and eat them too, make them of marshmallows or gumdrops, and use fresh leaves or green-gumdrop leaves for foliage.

Marshmallow flower: Using kitchen scissors, cut each marshmallow into five crosswise slices. Shape each slice into a petal, rounded on one end, somewhat pointed on the other, using your fingers to push and pull. Overlap the rounded ends and press together. Place a slice of small gumdrop, any color, in the center. If you wish, the edges of the flower petals may be dipped in colored sugar.

For leaves, roll a large green gumdrop thin between pieces of waxed paper or on a board, using granulated sugar to keep the gumdrop from sticking. Cut out leaves with a small leaf-shaped cutter or by following a cardboard pattern with a sharp knife.

You can make gumdrop flowers in the same way, rolling out big gumdrops of whatever color you like, cutting petal shapes and pressing them together, or rolling long, thin pieces of rolled-out gumdrops into roses. Candied fruit-slice gumdrops, just as they are, make pretty decorations, too; they are flavored with orange, lemon, and lime, and come in colors appropriate to the flavors.

Fruitful decoration ideas

Handsome cake decorations can be contrived of fruit—fresh or glacéed or candied—and, because all these fruits are so good to eat, they give an added dimension to the dessert. All fresh fruit should be put in place on the cake shortly before it is served, but the candied kind can be positioned in advance. Here are some suggestions to spur your imagination.

Ring the top of an angel food cake with whole fresh strawberries, standing on their stem ends, and repeat the circle on the cake plate at the base of the cake. Lemon-glaze a bundt cake and position standup half slices of lemon in the glaze in the low creases on top of the cake. Ice a fruitcake with a plain white glaze; halfway between the center and the edge of the cake, make a circle of red candied cherries. Make a second circle, about an inch nearer the edge, of green candied cherries, and use pieces of angelica to fan out from the second circle to the edge of the cake. Wreath a lemon-iced spice cake with a combination of candied ginger and pecan halves. Place them in a tight circle around the edge of the cake. To decorate a raisin cake, melt a jar of apricot preserves in a saucepan over low heat; stir in 2 to 3 tablespoons of water, depending on the consistency you want, and cook it for 1 minute. Let the glaze cool slightly, pour it over the cake, and let it set for half an hour. Decorate the top of the cake with snipped glacéed apricots, blanched almonds, and plump raisins in alternating strips.

Decorate the top of a light fruitcake with an opaque glaze. Heat 2 tablespoons of butter and 2 tablespoons of cream together until the butter is melted. Beat in 2 cups of confectioners sugar. Thin the mixture to a slow-pouring consistency by adding hot water. Spoon the glaze over the cake, letting some run down the sides. On the top, halfway between the center and the edge, build a Della Robbia wreath of halved candied cherries, candied orange and grapefruit peel, candied citron, ginger and angelica, and whole blanched almonds and pecan halves—in fact, use any nuts and/or candied or glacéed fruit that you have available. Place the pieces close together, alternating shapes and colors in any pattern that pleases your eye, letting a little of the white icing show through here and there. Don't try for neat edges—a lavish effect is what you're striving for—and don't cover the entire top of the cake; leave some frosting showing in the middle and around the outside edge.

Halved fresh cherries placed close together all over the top dress up both the looks and flavor of a square or rectangular chocolate cake; glaze the cherries with a little melted cherry jelly. Or top a sponge cake with peeled, sliced oranges, and spoon apricot glaze over the slices. Or omit the glaze, sprinkle the oranges lightly with white or brown sugar, and pass a bowl of dairy sour cream to top each serving of cake.

A cream-and-fruit combination is both pretty and delicious on almost any cake, but it is particularly good with the foam cakes. Split an angel food or sponge or chiffon cake into layers; fill between the layers and top the cake with sliced fresh strawberries or whole fresh raspberries mixed with sweetened whipped cream. (Use just enough whipped cream to bind the berries.)

Macaroons, marzipan, meringues

Almond paste is the magic ingredient of a dozen good things to be made in any home kitchen. You can make the paste yourself, if you like—any good general cookbook will tell you how—but almond paste of excellent quality can be purchased in cans or packages that keep for a long time on the pantry shelf. (An aside of cooking philosophy: If it cannot be bought, make it. If it can be bought, but is not as good as homemade, make it. *But* if the purchased form is as good as, or better than, the homemade variety, save your time and energy!)

Little almond macaroons—they offer a flavor delight with a texture that is both chewy and crunchy—make splendid decorations for a cake, enriching both its looks and flavor. Stud them all over the frosting or border the top and sides with them. The macaroons can be made in advance, but don't position them on the cake until shortly before serving it. They partner well with almost any flavor cake, but they are particularly good with chocolate. The following recipe will make enough macaroons to decorate a cake lavishly, still leaving a few left over for sampling.

ALMOND MACAROONS   3 dozen

1 (8-ounce) can or package almond paste	Few grains salt
	1 teaspoon vanilla extract
2 egg whites	1 cup sifted confectioners sugar

Grease a large baking sheet; dust lightly with flour and tap off excess. Preheat oven to 325° F. With fingers, break up almond paste into large bowl of electric mixer. Add egg whites, salt, and vanilla. Beat at low speed until mixture is smooth and well blended. Add sugar slowly, continuing to beat at low speed until a soft dough forms. Drop by scant teaspoonfuls onto prepared baking sheet (they spread very little in baking). Bake until light golden brown, about 20 minutes. Using a spatula, remove at once from baking sheet to wire racks.

Marzipan fruits (or vegetables, or almost any form you like) are also made with almond paste. They are a delicious and handsome decoration for almost any kind of cake—and, in their making, they give the home cook a chance to exercise her artistic talent. (Don't say you don't have any until you've tried—you'll be surprised.) This variation on the usual recipe produces a delicious, easy-to-handle result.

MARZIPAN   about 2 pounds

2 (8-ounce) cans or packages almond paste	Light corn syrup
	3¾ cups sifted confectioners sugar
1 (7-ounce) jar marshmallow cream	Assorted liquid food colorings
	Assorted colored sugars

With your fingers, crumble almond paste into a medium-size bowl. Blend in marshmallow cream and ¼ cup corn syrup. Stir in sufficient confectioners sugar to make a very stiff dough. Sprinkle remaining sugar on a board or marble slab; turn out almond paste mixture into sugar. Knead mixture until smooth and all sugar is worked in, 5 minutes or more.

To make marzipan fruits: Pinch off half-teaspoons of the mixture and mold it, with your fingers and between the palms of your hands, into small fruit shapes—apples, bananas, pears, oranges, lemons, limes,

112

peaches, strawberries, whatever. Place the shapes on waxed paper so that they do not touch each other; let them stand several hours, until dry. To decorate, mix small amounts of food coloring with equal amounts of water in small containers, such as custard cups. Using an artist's brush, brush small amounts of color on the marzipan fruits to tint. You can use two colors if you like—for example, add a light blush of red to the cheek of a golden peach. Or decorate with chocolate—draw a tip and stem end on a yellow banana, for example, using a food pick dipped in melted chocolate. Bits of angelica and whole cloves can be used as stems and leaves where you wish, and the fruits can be rolled in colored sugar when appropriate. For example, tint a strawberry a rich strawberry red, roll it in red sugar, and insert a whole clove for a stem. If you like, you can glaze the finished fruits (except those dipped in sugar): Let the food coloring dry, then brush the fruit with a glaze made of 1 tablespoon of light corn syrup diluted with ¾ teaspoon water.

If you are very fond of almond paste, use it to make a decorative frosting for a cake. Crumble the almond paste into a bowl and, using your fingers, work into it just enough unbeaten egg white to make it malleable. To color it, work in a little liquid food coloring, mixing well so that there will be no streaks in the finished product. A very pale green tint is traditional for almond-flavored foods; however, any pale color can be used. Sift confectioners sugar onto a board and roll out the almond paste to a size and shape that will cover the cake. (A patterned roller will give texture to the frosting.) Drape the almond paste mixture over the rolling pin and transfer it to the cake. Using your fingers, smooth it into place; cut off the excess frosting. Decorate the cake with blanched almonds, with marzipan fruits, or with almond-paste roses.

Almond-paste roses: Shape tinted almond-paste frosting (see above) into a roll about an inch in diameter. Cut the roll into 1-inch pieces; shape each piece into a ball. Shape each ball into a petal by placing it on a sheet of waxed paper and, using a metal spatula, smoothing the ball away from you into a petal shape that is ⅛ inch thick at the side nearest you and tapers to a very thin edge at the side away from you. Make petals of the remaining balls the same way, reserving one ball for the center of each flower. Mold that ball into a cone shape. Press the base (the thicker edge) of each petal gently but firmly around the cone, shaping the top petals in closely and gradually flaring the succeeding layers of petals out toward the base of the cone. Trim the bottom of each rose so that it will sit evenly on the cake. Or shape leaves from green-tinted paste and place them on the cake, then place the roses on top of the leaves.

If you choose, you may cover an almond-paste frosting with butter cream frosting, or with a glaze. (You can create a memorable dessert by covering a chocolate cake with almond-paste frosting, glazing it with chocolate, and decorating it with whole blanched almonds.) However, no other frosting is really needed. Almond-paste frosting is not difficult to handle and accommodates itself to unusual shapes with little trouble. For example, tint it pink and use it to frost a heart-shaped Valentine cake.

Small meringues—crispy pieces of air, as a child once described them—make lovely decorations when gently pressed into the smooth frosting of almost any except the dense kinds of cakes, such as pound cakes. Filled meringues and marguerites can also be used.

MERINGUES   about 3 dozen

2 egg whites   ⅔ cup sugar, divided
⅛ teaspoon salt

Cover a baking sheet with unglazed paper. Preheat oven to 225°F. In a medium bowl, beat egg whites with salt until they stand in soft peaks. Beat in ½ cup sugar, 2 tablespoons at a time. The mixture should be stiff enough to hold its shape, and the sugar should be completely dissolved. Using 2 teaspoons (or use a pastry bag fitted with a plain tube), shape mounds of the mixture, about 1 teaspoonful for each mound, on the paper-covered baking sheet. Space mounds about 1 inch apart. Sprinkle lightly with remaining sugar. Bake until crisp and just beginning to change color, about 50 minutes. Cool slightly, then remove from paper with a spatula. If they stick, moisten the underside of the paper slightly.

Filled meringues: Make the meringues slightly larger, and before baking, make an indentation in each one with the tip of a spoon. When they are cool, drop a small amount of either melted semisweet chocolate or fruit preserve (of any flavor you like) into the indentation.
Marguerites: Fold ½ cup finely chopped walnuts into the meringue mixture before shaping and baking.

Always store meringues, uncovered, in a dry place.

Here are two cakes that use meringue in place of the frosting itself. Both are beautiful and delicious, and both give the appearance of having been labored over long and lovingly. As a matter of fact, neither cake is difficult to make. The first, Daria's Torte, uses one mix for the cake and another for the filling.

DARIA'S TORTE

filling:
- 1 (3½-ounce) package vanilla
  pudding and pie filling mix
- 1 teaspoon vanilla extract
- ¼ cup heavy cream, whipped

cake:
- 1 (18½-ounce) package yellow
  cake mix
- 1 teaspoon vanilla extract

topping:
- 3 egg whites
- ⅔ cup superfine granulated sugar
- ½ cup sliced blanched almonds

Make the filling according to package directions, but use only 1½ cups milk. When cooked, stir in 1 teaspoon vanilla. Place a piece of plastic wrap directly on the pudding surface and refrigerate.

Make the cake according to package directions, adding one teaspoon vanilla along with the water. Pour batter into two buttered and floured 9-inch layer cake pans. Preheat oven to 350°F.

Make the topping by beating the egg whites until they form soft peaks. Add sugar, about 2 tablespoons at a time, beating until sugar is completely dissolved and mixture holds stiff peaks.

Gently spread the topping mixture over the cake batter, dividing it between the two pans and swirling the meringue in an attractive pattern. Sprinkle the almonds over one of the layers. Bake 25 to 30 minutes, or until the cake tests done with a cake tester or food pick. Cool in pans on racks 15 minutes. Remove layers from pans and let stand separately, on racks, until completely cold. Do not cover. While cake cools, fold whipped cream into pudding mixture and return it to refrigerator.

Complete the cake by placing the layer without the almonds on a serving plate, meringue side up. Spread it with filling and top it with second layer, almond–meringue side up. Serve at once. Leftovers may be refrigerated, but the meringue will lose its crispness.

DARIA'S OUTSIDE-INSIDE CAKE

outside:
- 4 egg whites
- ¼ teaspoon cream of tartar
- 1 cup sugar

- 1 (1-ounce) square unsweetened
  chocolate, grated
- ½ cup finely chopped pecans

inside:
- ½ cup butter or margarine
- 1 cup sugar
- 1½ teaspoons vanilla extract
- 4 egg yolks

- 2 cups sifted cake flour
- 3 teaspoons baking powder
- ½ teaspoon salt
- ¾ cup milk

To make the outside: Butter a 10-inch tube pan; line the bottom with waxed paper. In the large mixer bowl, beat egg whites with cream of tartar at medium-high speed of mixer until soft peaks form. Add sugar, 2 tablespoons at a time, beating at high speed until sugar is dissolved and mixture forms stiff peaks. Fold in chocolate and pecans. Spread mixture evenly over bottom and 3½ inches up sides and tube of prepared pan. Set aside.

To make the inside: Preheat oven to 325°F. Wash the bowl and beaters well. In the large mixer bowl, cream sugar, butter, and vanilla together until fluffy. Add egg yolks, one at a time, beating well after each addition. Sift together cake flour, baking powder, and salt. Add to creamed mixture alternately with milk, beating well after each addition. Spoon very carefully into meringue-lined cake pan. Bake 55 to 60 minutes, or until the cake tests done. Cool in pan, *not* inverted, on rack 20 minutes. Using a thin-bladed knife, carefully loosen cake around sides and center tube. Invert cake on cake rack to cool completely, carefully peeling off waxed paper if it has adhered to cake.

The fearless cake maker

As you can see, it's possible for you to make and serve truly handsome cakes, beautifully decorated, without ever holding a pastry bag in your hand. You can make cakes with style, serve them with flair, and never be ashamed that the very thought of the more complicated ways of cake decorating sends you into a panic.

No one need ever know. But wouldn't you like to try, just to see if it's as difficult as it looks?

Cakes for the Somewhat-Skilled

Elaborately decorated cakes require time, effort, and skill on the part of the decorator. Whether the cake is as exquisite as an old master or a colorful mishmash in dubious taste, a great deal of work has gone into it. The cake itself is usually rather plain, of a texture sturdy enough to hold up the production that crowns it. It is that production that represents the patience and know-how.

Only you know whether you can provide the requisite patience. The know-how can be learned, but you must be prepared to invest time in acquiring the necessary skills, and yet more time in practicing them in order to realize a cake you'll be proud of. You must, of course, bring to the project a certain amount of latent dexterity and coordination. If you've never been able to wrap a package so that the post office will accept it, if you've never been able to hem a dress so that it's even all around, forget cake decorating and scout around for some other craft.

No matter how skillful, dexterous, and coordinated you are, it is doubtful that you can, from reading a book, learn how to make the elaborate kind of decorated cake that is produced by a professional cake decorator. That know-how must be demonstrated to you, and practiced in the presence of an instructor who can correct, encourage, and guide you. In other words, you'll have to take a course in cake decoration. Such classes are available almost everywhere. But a word of caution. You must choose a school of cake decorating as carefully as you would a school that teaches any other craft—painting, pottery, needlework. In other words, examine the products of both pupils and teacher before you decide to enroll. Skill is of course important in this craft, but there is more. Taste counts, too. Cakes produced by some professional decorators are monstrosities. Happily, other decorators turn out cakes that are exceedingly beautiful. Be sure you get one of the latter for your teacher.

If, on the other hand, your ambition is simply to acquire the fundamentals in order to make attractive cakes that you can offer guests with pride and pleasure, you can learn the basic skills from a book—this one—and go on from there.

A worker needs tools

One needs more than a few food picks and a couple of spoons to produce even the simplest patterns, borders, flowers, and such. A beginner, however, does not need a complete set of the more than a hundred decorating tubes available, plus the whole world of gadgets offered in cake-decorating-equipment catalogs. A beginner's set of basic tubes and bags, and a couple of spatulas—one rubber, one metal—are really all you need to get started. If you like what you accomplish with these elementary tools, you can go on to bigger things. If not, give the tools to someone else and let her try her hand—not all of us are cut out to be cake decorators.

Parchment paper is a useful substitute for pastry bags. Most professional pastry chefs use cones—they call them cornets—made of this material; a separate cone can be made for each color frosting used, and disposed of after use. Pastry bags of old, which were generally made of unbleached muslin, were difficult to wash; it was a task that required true dedication to the art. Nowadays, however, plastic-lined bags are available and are a relative breeze to clean. Transparent plastic bags, too, can be easily washed and reused a (limited) number of times.

To achieve basic cake decorating you should be able to set yourself up with appropriate equipment for about ten dollars. Basic sets of tubes come with booklets of step-by-step instructions, with pictures—a definite advantage. Everything you need is for sale in good kitchenware departments of department stores, in gourmet cookware shops, or by mail. (See Tools of the Trade.)

A novice needs practice

No matter how enchanted you may be with the idea of cake decorating and no matter how dexterous you are by nature, you are not likely to meet with instant success. This is one craft that requires considerable practice before you can claim any degree of expertise, so don't be immediately discouraged.

To get the feel of using decorator frosting, invest in a few tubes of ready-prepared icing—these are for sale in all supermarkets of reasonable size. At the same time, buy a packaged set of tips and a nail (a miniature turntable, used for forming flowers off the cake), which you'll find for sale close to the tubes of icing. An instruction booklet comes with the set. Read it and then—working on a piece of waxed paper, not on a cake —practice some of the elementary forms of borders and flowers. In the same area of the supermarket (usually near the cake and frosting mixes and/or the flavoring extracts) there are smaller tubes of translucent gel in assorted colors. Use these to practice printing and script writing.

Alternatively, practice with a pastry bag and tubes filled with prepared instant mashed potatoes. (Make the potato mixture somewhat thicker than you'd serve for supper.) This will familiarize you with the bag and tubes, though it is admittedly not as much fun as squeezing colored icings and gels from the tubes.

Whichever way you choose, practice until you can produce the shape and size you are trying for, learning as you go how to guide the tip of the tube, how much pressure to use, and—above all—how to be neat. When you've learned how to produce leaves that are separate from one another and have an identifiable shape, flowers that are not simply blobs connected by unsightly strings of frosting, borders that are attractive and maintain a straight line, you're ready to go on to the real thing.

To start with: a cake

A high rather than a flat cake accepts decorating better—layers (round or square) or a cake baked in a tube or springform or bundt pan or in a fancy mold, such as a turk's head. If you have some special effect in mind, bake the cake in an ovenproof container of the shape you desire (such as a mixing bowl) instead of a pan. Later, treat yourself to special pans, if you like—they produce handsome cakes, whether ornamented with decorator's frostings or frosted and decorated simply in one of the manners suggested in Cakes for All-Thumbs Decorators. Such pans come in a variety of shapes and sizes: tiers, graduated layers, and shapes ranging from a simple heart to an elaborate animal or as way out as a set of bowling pins and ball. Most such pans, or sets of pans, come with instructions that will guide you in planning the amount of cake batter needed to fill them.

In learning decorating skills, however, don't overreach. Start with a simple shape. If you find that cake decorating is a craft you're going to enjoy and one you're going to be good at, then branch out and try your hand at fancier forms.

Second step: the cake must be frosted

On a cake for which the frosting itself is the major decoration, frosting is usually piled high and swirled on. However, a cake that is going to be ornamented with decorator's icing must offer a smooth surface for the decorator to work on.

Almost any frosting you favor can be smoothed, then decorated. Even the rolled-out almond-paste frosting (see Index) works very well. Here are two good frostings that can be used both to ice the cake and then, with bag and tube, to decorate it.

Butter cream: Place ⅔ cup of cold, firm butter or margarine into the small bowl of an electric mixer. Beat the butter several minutes until it is creamy. Add sifted confectioners sugar, ½ cup at a time, beating well after each addition, until you have added 4 cups. Add 1 teaspoon of vanilla extract. Beat in 2 to 3 tablespoons of cool milk or cream, a little at a time, until the icing is of the consistency you want. Beat the icing well again. Refrigerate it in an airtight container; beat it once more before using it.

This icing can be tinted any color you like. It has a rich, creamy texture. If you want a snow-white butter cream, substitute white vegetable shortening for the butter, and add butter flavoring. A speck of blue food coloring, thoroughly blended in, will make the white whiter. But be sure it's only a speck.

A boiled icing, made by the following method, will be light and fluffy, yet stand up very well and hold a shape. Have everything you use scrupulously clean—even the least bit of grease can break down this type of icing.

Boiled icing: In a heavy saucepan, combine 2 cups of sugar, ½ cup of water, and ¼ teaspoon of cream of tartar. Set a candy thermometer in place; bring the mixture to a temperature of 240°F. Brush the sides of the pan with a pastry brush dipped in warm water when the mixture begins to boil, and again when a temperature of about 220°F. is reached. (This prevents sugar crystals from forming.) While the mixture cooks, beat 4 egg whites at high speed of an electric mixer for 7 minutes. Continuing to beat, gradually pour in the hot sugar mixture; continue to beat for 3 minutes at high speed. Turn the speed to low; gradually add 1½ cups of sifted confectioners sugar; return the speed to high and beat 5 minutes more.

The butter-cream icing will make a fine frosting and filling for your

119

cake and can also be used with bags and tubes to pipe well-shaped flowers and borders. The boiled icing can frost and fill a cake and can be used for piping borders, but it is not firm enough for making flowers. (A boiled icing for any use can be made with meringue powder, a decorator's ingredient you may want to experiment with if you decide that cake decorating is indeed for you.) Both recipes produce icings of a medium consistency. The medium consistency produces a peak that stands about ¾ inch high on a spatula that has been dipped into it. To thin it, as for printing or writing messages, add a few drops of milk; for a stiffer consistency, add confectioners sugar, a little at a time.

The cake to be frosted should be completely cooled—refrigerate it for a while to be sure. If it is a layer cake, fill and assemble it according to the directions in Cakes for All-Thumbs Decorators. Seal the top against loose crumbs by brushing it with hot apricot glaze (1 cup of strained apricot jam, heated) or by coating the top with a very thin layer of the frosting you are going to use. In either case, let the coating cool and set before continuing.

Frost the sides of the cake first (with strips of waxed paper beneath it to protect the plate, remember?) in long, even, upward strokes from bottom to top. Build the frosting just a little above the top of the cake. Now spoon a heap of icing on the cake top and spread it out, blending it neatly with the built-up edges.

Third step: the surface must be smoothed

Create a backdrop for your decorating by smoothing the surface of the cake with a spatula dipped in hot water. Place it flat on the cake top, from the center to the edge. Holding the spatula perfectly still and pressing down lightly, slowly and carefully rotate the cake plate. Discard any frosting that has clung to the spatula; don't try to return it to the top of the cake.

You can also smooth the top of the cake with a strip of stiff cardboard, shaped like a ruler. Hold it by both ends, tipped very slightly toward you, and pull it straight across the cake. It will remove excess icing and smooth the cake's top surface.

Finally, smooth the sides of the cake. Again, dip your spatula in hot water. Holding it flat against the side of the cake, rotate the cake plate a full turn with your other hand.

And there you are, ready to apply the icing decorations.

Getting your tools ready

Now that you are going to use a pastry bag and/or parchment-paper cone, you need to know how to prepare and fill them.

Opposite: Frosted cake with butter-cream flowers and basket-weave lattice pattern, decorator's icing and tools

·To make a parchment-paper cone: From parchment paper, cut a triangle 11 inches on the long side, 8 inches on each of the two shorter sides. Hold the triangle, long side at the bottom, with the thumb and forefinger of your right hand. With your left hand, bring the lower left-hand point up to meet the point at the top, rolling half the paper into a cone shape. Bring the lower righthand corner around the outside of the cone shape and up to the point, so that you have two thicknesses of paper on each side of the cone. You now have a complete cone. Fasten the top of the cone with tape or staples. Fold the remaining point down into the cone so that the rim is even. Using scissors, cut ¾ of an inch off of the bottom point of the cone. Slip a decorator tube into the cone so that it protrudes through the hole. Fill the cone halfway with decorator icing. Fold the top in a "diaper fold"—first crease and turn the two outer sides in to meet at the middle, then fold the resulting peak down over those points. This will keep the frosting from coming out at you—rather than through the tube—as you squeeze the cone.

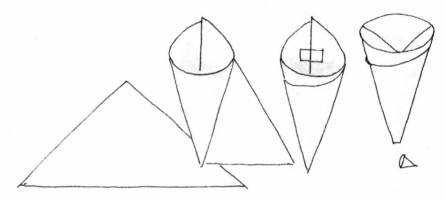

To fill a decorating bag: You simply drop the tube you are going to use into one type of bag. Other kinds have a coupler (an advantage, because you can change tubes as you work if you wish) onto which special threaded tubes can be fastened. Drop either the tube itself, or the coupler, into the bag. If using a coupler, attach the tube to it. Turn over the top third of the tube, on the outside, like a cuff. Fill the bag with icing almost to the top of the cuff. Then unfold the cuff and either twist it tightly or use the diaper fold to keep the icing from squeezing out in the wrong direction.

Learning to hold the pastry tube

The angle at which you hold the bag is important. It changes, depending on the kind of decorating you are going to do.

Fit a bag or cone with a #3 tube, and fill the bag with icing of medium consistency. Hold the bag in your right hand, using the fingers of that hand to press out the icing firmly and steadily. Use your left hand only to guide the bag and keep it steady. And remember—practice before you decorate a cake to be seen by any eyes but your own.

For borders, both around the bottom of a cake and around the top edge of it, hold the bag at a 45-degree angle to the surface. Try a zigzag border, making short up-and-down motions with the bag, spacing the zigzags close together or far apart, as you like, but keeping them uniform. Then try a curving border, slowly moving the bag to make long, sweeping curves. Practice until you can keep the thickness of the icing and the spacing of the pattern uniform, and until, at the end of a piece of decoration, you can stop squeezing, lift the bag away in one motion, and make a clean break.

With the same tube, change the position of your hand so that it is almost palm up—so that the bag is as nearly as possible parallel to the surface on which you're working. This is the position for making lines (flower stems, for instance) and for both printing and script writing. With the bag in this position, practice making short parallel lines—horizontal, vertical, slanted—striving for uniform thickness and length, and neatly cut-off ends. Then try some printed letters of the alphabet—C is the easiest to start with—again trying for uniformity and neatness.

Try making a decorative border with tube #14, using the same consistency of icing and the same position of your hands and the bag in relation to the surface. Move slowly, squeezing with uniform pressure, making very short up-and-down zigzags. Try to make the border even in width and thickness and to break off cleanly at the end.

Using tube #3 (but this time with icing softened with a few drops of water), practice the scallop effect that is called stringwork. Raise the cake surface you are working on to eye level. Point the bag straight at it, with the tip of the tube at a 90-degree angle to the work surface. Squeeze lightly to attach the icing, then gently pull the bag toward you, letting a string of icing drop down about 1½ inches; loop it up, attach it to the surface, even with the other end, and repeat the process until you have a series of stringwork scallops. Never move the bag down with the icing—let the string of icing drop, then attach it to the cake. You can make a series of single scallops or a series of doubles (make one set first, then the second below it); make the second set deeper than the first. Later, try making scallops with icings of two different colors. Cover the points where the two sets of scallops attach to the cake with little rings or squiggles of icing.

Practicing simple shapes

Turn a baking sheet upside down. Drop a few dots of icing on it, then lay a piece of waxed paper on top—the frosting dots will hold it in place.

Prepare a pastry bag with a #6 tube and icing that is slightly stiffer than medium consistency. Hold the bag straight up, at a 90-degree angle to the waxed paper. Touch the tube lightly to the paper. Squeeze, raising the tube upward with the icing as it begins to mound. Stop the pressure and break the icing off neatly. You have produced a dot. Light pressure will give you a small dot, medium pressure a dot of medium size. Try more dots—of varying sizes, or all the same size neatly spaced, or all the same size with their edges touching. Try for roundness, for uniform shape. Try heavy pressure for larger, fatter dots—still keeping them round and neat.

Using tube #17, with the same slightly stiffer consistency of icing and the bag held in the same position, do some stars—again, vary their size, place them singly or close together in a row. Try for neatness and uniformity. Hold the tube in place just long enough to form the star, then break away cleanly. Again, light pressure will give you a small star, medium pressure a star of medium size, heavy pressure a large star.

Using the same tube, same icing, same position, make some rosettes—basic stars but, as you pipe them, swirl the bag up and away in a circular motion. Try various sizes. Try a row of rosettes placed close together, sides touching. Remember that you're working for uniformity, neatness, and clean breaks. Remember too that you can control the size of the rosettes by the amount of pressure you use in squeezing the icing out of the bag.

Shells and garlands

Using slightly stiffened icing and tube #21, make a shell—one of the decorations that requires you to use varying pressure during its production. Start by touching the tip of the tube lightly to the waxed paper. Squeeze heavily, hesitating long enough to make a built-up, fanned-out shape that is the base of the shell. Let up the pressure and pull your hand down sharply, drawing the icing out to a point. Make a clean break. Try another. Then try different pressures for shells of varied size—lighter for small ones, heavier for big ones. Try a shell border, piping each shell on the tail of the one ahead of it.

You can use this combination of light and heavy pressure to make garland shapes with various tubes, starting lightly, building up pressure for a thicker and wider icing in the middle, and tailing off with a lighter pressure at the other end. A series of such shapes, one touching another, made with a very tight zigzag motion, produces a handsome garland. You might try tube #14 to practice this.

Now try combining borders, garlands, stringwork, shells, and stars to create patterns, testing your taste and artistry as well as your skill. Combine colors and patterns until you get the feel of making such combinations, the hang of what goes with what to make a pretty pattern.

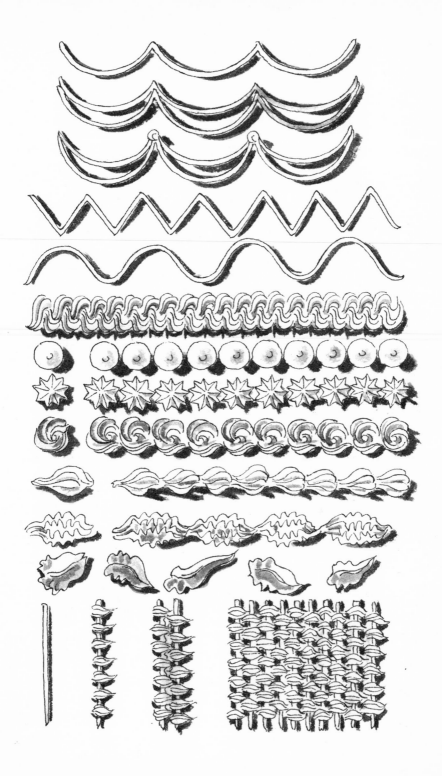

Leaves and flowers

Prepare the pastry bag with tube #67 and softened icing tinted green. Touch the tip of the tube to the working surface; squeeze the tube to build up the base of the leaf, then gradually pull it away, relaxing the pressure as you do. Stop pressing and lift the tube away to finish the leaf with a sharp point. To make a somewhat rippled leaf, jiggle your hand as you squeeze, either continuously or at intervals. Try to suit the leaf to the flower if you are decorating with flowers—that is, long and thin, long and thick, short and stubby, and so on. Pipe the stems for the leaves with a #3 tube.

The leaf tube will also pipe a very handsome ruffled border. Simply keep going, squeezing with medium speed and pressure, for as long as you like, rather than lifting the tube from the surface.

Drop flowers are made on waxed paper and later transferred to the cake that is already prepared for them—that is, leaves and stems have been piped in place, and any other decorating has already been done. Drop flowers are made with a different kind of frosting, called Royal Icing, which hardens to a cementlike (and, be warned, virtually tooth-breaking) consistency. Drop flower tubes of various shapes (making flowers of various kinds) come in standard, large, and extra-large sizes. The flowers they make are attractive to a certain extent, but they have a no-give look to them, and violate the principle that decorations ought to be edible. Once you become sufficiently proficient with the use of bags and tubes, however, you can—using these same tubes—drop flowers of edible butter-cream icing right on the surface of the cake. Other flowers made of butter cream, using various flower tubes, can also be dropped on the cake or made in advance and frozen for later use. Making flowers can be a somewhat lengthy business, so by making them in advance, you simplify the decorating of the cake and shorten the time it takes. Freezing makes them easier to handle.

A second type of made-in-advance flower is produced on a nail, a tiny turntable held in one hand. Such flowers have the advantage of being full-round, like a real flower, rather than half-round, as they are when made on a flat surface. All sorts of flowers, some of them very handsome indeed, can be made on a nail. By the time you've reached a degree of proficiency that induces you to try this kind of flower-making, you'll want to buy the proper tubes, nails of several sizes (there are special nails for some flowers, such as lilies), and an instruction book that spells out for you step by step (with an illustration for each step) how these flowers are made. Have recourse to your nearest reliable house-wares department, or to one of the mail-order houses listed in Tools of the Trade. The catalogs of these firms offer every imaginable device for helping you become a dedicated cake decorator.

Two colors, three colors, a whole rainbow

It is possible to vary colors and patterns of flowers and borders by using two or more tubes, or two or more colors of icing. But it's also possible to achieve this with one bag of icing and one tube, through a method known as striping. There are several ways of doing this.

Brush striping: This method is used when you want a fairly sharp color contrast, with part of the decoration in a deep color, part in a pale one. Use a parchment decorating cone for this. With an artist's brush, paint a vertical stripe of undiluted paste color on the inside of the cone. If you want two added colors or a multicolor effect, paint the cone with two or more stripes of different colors. Then fill the cone with white icing, or a pale pastel tint of one of the colors with which you are striping. When you pipe, you will produce two-color or three-or-more-color borders, flowers, or whatever, depending on the tube you use.

Spatula striping: This method is used when you want two- or three-tone pastels. With a spatula, place a vertical stripe of pastel-tinted icing inside a decorator cone. If you want a three-color effect, place two stripes, one a bit darker than the other. Then fill the cone with white icing, or the palest pastel tint, to pipe two- or three-shade borders or flowers with shaded petals.

Another way of adding a second color is with an atomizer. Fill its bowl with water tinted with liquid food coloring. Spray the color onto the decorations you have already made on a sheet of waxed paper or on a nail. Be sure to dry the sprayed decorations thoroughly before placing them on the cake. And take it easy here—a little goes a long way. Don't wash your decorations away in a flood when a light mist is all you need.

A green-and-yellow basket

Icing basketry can be very attractive. It's a skill that requires some work, however, and you'll need to practice before working directly on a cake. Once you've got the hang of it, you can do anything from making a small flower-filled basket on top of a cake to covering an entire cake with woven-basketry icing.

Weaving a basket: Fit a bag or parchment cone with a #3 tube and a second bag with a #15 tube. Fill both bags with icing, using one color or two different shades of the same color; if you're using two shades, use the darker one in the bag with the #3 tube. Invert a baking sheet and drop a few dots of icing on the bottom. Place a piece of waxed paper on top of the dots and press it into the dots so that it will stay in place. Using the #3 tube, pipe a vertical line of icing about 6 inches long. Using the #15 tube, pipe horizontal rows of icing across the vertical line of icing, spacing them about ¼ inch apart and keeping them all the same length. Now pipe a second vertical line at the end of the horizontal rows; pipe more horizontal rows over it, starting each at the first vertical line and placing each midway between two of the first horizontal rows. Keep these rows roughly the same length as the first ones. Continue to make vertical lines and horizontal rows (alternating their placement as described above) and, as you'll quickly see, you will have created a woven, basketlike effect. It may not be beautifully neat the first time, but practice will improve your technique until you're ready to decorate a cake or ice a whole basket cake. Or ice cupcake baskets all in one color and cover their tops with icing flowers in a variety of shapes and colors.

Tubes and more tubes

Decorator's tubes come in a multitude of patterns and, usually, in a number of variations—generally variations in size—of each pattern, so that once you've learned how to use the tubes, you can produce virtually an infinite variety of designs. Each tube has its own number and, fortunately, these numbers are the same from maker to maker. Here is a list of the most-often-used tubes to guide you in making a selection.

Numbers 1 through 12—plain tubes with openings of various sizes; the smaller numbers have the smaller openings; lines, dots, strings, and so on.

Numbers 13 through 22—open star tubes; for star shapes of various sizes, as well as for a number of borders.

Numbers 23 through 35—closed star tubes; for stars, shells, lettering.

Numbers 41 through 43—double-line tubes; for parallel lines, crisscross, lattice patterns; small, medium, and large.

Numbers 44 through 48, with variations—plain and fancy ribbon tubes; bows, borders, ribbons, knots, and some basketry.

Numbers 49 through 54—aster tubes for asters; also writing, lettering, small buds, and attractive scrolls.

Numbers 55 through 58—oval tubes; scrolls, borders, stems, and some flowers.

Numbers 59 through 61, with variations—flower tubes; for apple blossoms, dahlias, pansies, small roses, and wild roses.

Numbers 62 through 64—fancy border tubes; for creating handsome borders that are more complicated to look at than to make.

Numbers 65 through 70—leaf tubes; for large and small leaves, flat or standing.

Numbers 71 through 78—combination leaf/border tubes; two-sided, make leaves with one side, borders with the other; various sizes, various combinations of patterns.

Numbers 79 through 81—flower tubes; for narcissus, daffodils, lilies of the valley, and some "fantasy" flowers whose patterns originate in the decorator's mind, rather than in nature.

Numbers 82 through 85—square tubes; to produce four-sided beads, dots, loops, and scallops.

Numbers 86 through 88—border tubes; for many handsome effects, depending on the decorator's imagination.

Number 89—triple-line tube; pipes three parallel lines at once; for lines, cross-hatching, woven patterns, and basketry.

Numbers 94, 95—french leaf tubes; for intricate borders, special-effect leaves, and delicate fernlike designs.

Number 96—drop-flower tube; quick/easy individual flat flowers.

Number 97—full-bloom rose tube; position in which bag is held produces tight center and unfolding petals.

Number 98—shell tube; for separate shells or shells joined for borders.

Numbers 99, 100—different-design borders (depending on how the bag is held).

Numbers 101 through 104—flower tubes; for making flowers, such as violets, carnations, and poppies, directly on the cake surface.

Number 105—border tube; several variations, depending on the position in which the bag is held.

Those listed are the standard tubes, but there are many others designed for special uses, such as large pastry tubes, french cruller tubes, candleholder tubes, tubes to make various kinds of drop flowers and extra-large drop flowers, extra-large rose and leaf tubes, and many more. All the tubes listed can be purchased separately; often they can be found in sets of related tubes, such as a set of ten different drop-flower tubes, or in sets of six or ten or more various-purpose tubes for beginners.

Cautionary note—wash the tubes as soon as you're through working with them. They're something of a nuisance to clean in any event, but if the frosting in them gets crusty, it's difficult to clean them out. A specially designed brush is available to help in getting tubes tidy.

Added touches

Sometimes there are effects you want but simply can't get with the use of a tube alone. A food pick can add striations to a small too-plain area. A gadget called a decorator's comb can make neat parallel lines or a checked or diamond pattern on a large plain surface. A cotton swab dipped in water—be light-fingered!—can sometimes tidy up slippages. And an artist's brush dipped in full-strength or diluted food coloring can add notes of contrast, such as the small lines that help delineate the "face" of a pansy.

Take the weather into consideration when you decorate; icings need to be stiffer on a humid day than on a dry one. If it's raining buckets, hold off if you can until it clears up.

Planning plays a big part

Before you begin to decorate a cake you need to map out your strategy and get yourself organized. Plan your decoration in detail—preferably with paper and pencil instead of in your mind's eye—rather than just having a general notion of what you want to do. Without an advance plan, you may find yourself without room on the cake for "Happy Father's Day" or, worse, the top of the cake might look like a florist's trash barrel at the end of the day. Decorations are important, but remember that plain areas serve for contrast and point up the decorations. If a birthday cake is going to have candles, determine in advance where they're going to go, so that they won't look like an afterthought. If the cake is going to carry a message, plot it out to make sure you have room for all of it. If you're a novice, lightly draw the message in the frosting with a food pick first, to make certain that all the characters are the proper size and that they don't run up- or downhill or trail off the edge.

Have your decorator icing prepared in advance, divided up, tinted, and ready to use. Lay out the tubes you're going to need. If you're using parchment-paper cones, make enough of them in advance for each of the colors and/or for each tube you'll be using. Set out cone holders or glasses to hold the tubes while you're not using them. And if you're expecting the children home from school soon, postpone your artistic endeavors until you've been told all about today's show-and-tell or what that wonderful boy in English said to your adolescent daughter. Give everyone a snack, send the thundering herd on its way, *then* start decorating.

Other times, other techniques

Perhaps you like the concept of cake decorating and are reasonably dexterous, but don't have idea one about patterns. Help is at hand—buy a book or books, or go to the library and do some research. All sorts of patterns, for decorating all sorts of cakes, are available—for everything from a cake simply garlanded with a few flowers to those that look more as if a contractor rather than a home cook had produced them. All have step-by-step, tube-by-tube instructions. And if that kind of aid is still not enough, there are stencils to be had—simply press the stencil lightly into the frosting, remove it, and follow the imprinted lines with the bag and tube. Books and stencils, along with everything else you need or might even think you need, are available from firms that specialize in materials for both amateur and professional cake decorators.

If you should decide that all these bags and tubes are not for you, or perhaps just need a change of pace, experiment with a decorating technique known as glaze painting. One of the cake-decorating equipment firms calls it "color flow" and offers all sorts of patterns for it, from simple to extremely elaborate, as well as packaged "color flow" icing mix. All this equipment isn't necessary, however, unless or until you've decided to go in for glaze painting on a large scale.

You'll need a flat cake—one baked in a 9-inch-square pan is a good size for your first attempt—a batch of ornamental icing, one bag or cone fitted with a plain tube, such as a #3, and a pattern. Draw the pattern on a piece of paper exactly the size of the cake top, then cut out each piece, as if you were cutting up a jigsaw puzzle. Choose a simple pattern for your first attempt—perhaps a scene that includes an expanse of grass, a sky with a cloud in it, and a small, simply shaped house with a tree beside it. Make all these patterns sturdy-looking—with no thin lines and intricate curves. If you're in doubt about your artistic ability, simply divide the 9-inch square of paper into various shapes, some large, some small, for your first effort.

Place the cake on a plate, bottom-side up. Spread a thin layer of frosting over the cake and smooth it. Cut the pattern you have made into separate parts, following the outline of each pattern piece. Reassemble the pattern on top of the cake, and draw around each piece with a food pick. Remove the patterns. Using a #3, #4, or any plain tube, pipe ornamental icing (tinted or not, as you wish) around all the edges of each section. Allow it to dry completely. Add warm water to the remaining frosting, a few drops at a time, to make a glaze consistency. To test its consistency, take up a spoonful of the icing, then drop it back into the bowl; it is the proper consistency when the portion dropped back flows and disappears into the main portion in a second or two.

This is your glaze. Divide it into as many portions as there will be colors in your pattern; tint each portion. Gently spoon each color icing into its place in the pattern, separated by the dried piped-on lines of icing. Allow it to dry. After the glazes have dried, you can pipe additional ornaments on if you wish—such as door and window outlines on a house, eyes and mouth on a face, and so on.

The following recipe for ornamental icing to use in glaze painting provides a sufficient amount to practice with first, then to frost and decorate your cake.

Ornamental icing: Into the large bowl of an electric mixer, sift through a very fine sieve 1 (1-pound) package of confectioners sugar and 1 teaspoon of cream of tartar. Add 6 unbeaten egg whites and 1 teaspoon of vanilla or almond extract. With the mixer set at low speed, combine the ingredients; turn the mixer to high speed and beat the mixture until it is so stiff that a knife drawn through it leaves a clean-cut path. If it is necessary, beat in more sugar (it may be needed especially on damp days). Use the icing as it is for piping; thin it as directed for glaze painting.

Sugar molding is another cake decorating technique that can be used instead of, or to augment, piping with bag and tubes. It's simple and easy. The ingredients are already in your kitchen, but you must purchase the molds. They are available in an almost infinite variety of shapes—bells, crosses, animals, children's favorite cartoon characters, flowers, stars, whatever—in stores that sell decorating materials or by mail.

The sugar mixture can be tinted as you make it and/or ornamented with decorator's icing piped or spread on after the mold is dry. Here are two sugar combinations from which to make molds; they seem to work equally well—use whichever suits you.

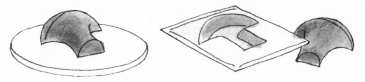

Sugar–water mixture: Into a bowl, measure 2 cups of granulated sugar. Add 4 teaspoons of water (and food coloring, if desired); mix and knead the mixture by hand until the sugar is uniformly moistened. If you require a large amount, double, triple, or quadruple these proportions. Pack the mixture solidly into the mold; scrape off any excess with a knife or spatula. Unmold it at once by placing a piece of cardboard over the open side of the mold; turn both upside down; lift the mold off. A mold will air dry as hard as a sugar cube in about 5 hours, or you can bake it for 5 minutes in a 200° F. oven. If you wish, white and tinted sugar mixtures, or two different tinted mixtures, may be combined in one mold.

Sugar–egg mixture: In a bowl, combine 4 cups of granulated sugar and 1 egg white (and food coloring, if desired). Combine and knead the mixture by hand until it is well blended. Pack it into molds as above; unmold, dry, and then decorate it, if desired.

Sometimes whipped cream, rather than frosting, is the just-right finishing touch for a cake. It can be sweetened and flavored or not as you choose; either way, it can be tinted a delicate pastel with food coloring if you like. Rather than simply spooning it on, pipe it on in an attractive design, using a pastry bag or cone and any tube whose pattern suits your purpose. A cake with a whipped cream topping should be served at once or refrigerated until serving time. If you are going to hold a cream-decorated cake for more than an hour or so, stabilize the whipped cream so that your pretty piped pattern won't begin to droop.

Stabilized whipped cream: In a small bowl, soften 1 teaspoon of unflavored gelatin in 2 tablespoons of cold water. Measure 1 cup of heavy cream; remove 3 tablespoons of the cream and scald it. Add the scalded cream to the gelatin, stirring until the gelatin is dissolved. Refrigerate the mixture until it is thickened but not set. Beat it until frothy. Whip the remaining cream; add a few grains of salt, 2 tablespoons of confectioners sugar, and ½ teaspoon of vanilla extract. Fold in the gelatin mixture. Place the cream mixture in the prepared bag or cone and pipe it on the cake. Refrigerate the cake until serving time and, of course, refrigerate any leftovers. If desired, 1 (6-ounce) package of semisweet chocolate pieces can be melted, cooled slightly, and folded into the cream for chocolate whipped cream.

A kitchenful of shapes and sizes

As well as the cake pans in various shapes suggested earlier, form cake pans are available. The difference between these and the shape pans is that the forms generally come in two parts; half the batter is baked in each part and the finished halves are fastened together with frosting. The whole is then frosted and decorated and the result is a full-round, standup figure—of a puppy, a teddy bear, an old-fashioned train engine, an Easter lamb, a ball, an egg, a bell, a tree, or almost anything else you might fancy. These pans, complete with instructions for batter and for decorating, are available in shops selling quality cookware or by mail (see Tools of the Trade).

Any and all of these form cakes, particularly those that will please children, can be delightfully decorated with frostings in appropriate colors, with chocolate or sugar molds, with candies and/or nuts, with plain or tinted coconut, and in dozens of other ways.

Work that's play

Once you're into cake decorating, you'll find that one idea sparks another, one technique you learn makes the next easier to master. There's a rewarding sense of satisfaction in the work (and it is work) as you do it, and you can be justly proud when you have learned to produce handsome cakes.

Cake decorating is a skill that enhances the desserts you serve to guests. You can consider it a hobby, a craft, or—if it turns out that this is something you do very well—you can turn it into a part-time or a full-time occupation. There are women everywhere who have made the decorating of cakes for their less dexterous friends and neighbors a profitable enterprise. Or you might decide to share your skill, on a volunteer basis or as a paid teacher, by giving classes in the art.

Even if you decorate just for fun, to please yourself and your family and the people you invite to your home, it's a skill worth developing, one in which you can take pride and pleasure.

Decorating Cookies

From little buttery melt-in-your-mouth one-bite cookies for a tea tray, through sturdy peanut butter crisscrossed cookies to greet the children with when they come home from school, to fat-and-sassy gingerbread families for the holidays, cookies are fun to make, a pleasure to decorate, and a joy to serve to your family and friends. Most kinds are easy to make —there's nothing chancy in their baking—and decorating them doesn't tax the ingenuity or the skill of the average home cook.

When children want to help you cook, cookies are the place to begin. They love to roll and shape and cut them—and what does it matter if the finished products are a bit tough from too much flour, the designs a trifle lopsided, the kitchen a shambles? Cooking together is a learning experience, not only for the children but also for you. You may discover in a son or daughter some traits (persistence? latent artistic ability? a tendency to give in too easily to frustration?) that you didn't know existed, that you may want to develop or discourage.

The easy way out

For the day-to-day job of keeping the cookie jar filled, nothing beats refrigerator cookies. (Icebox cookies, they used to be called, and still are sometimes.) They're easy to make, needing only to be quickly sliced and briefly baked—indeed, a roll can always be kept ready in the refrigerator. The dough can be vanilla-, chocolate-, lemon-, spice-, almond-, or butter-scotch-flavored; it can be left plain or have nuts, raisins, currants, chocolate pieces, or candied fruit peel (all of these chopped fine) incorporated into it. The sliced cookies can be left as they are or sprinkled with plain or colored sugar or with nuts before being baked, or the finished cookies can be frosted or glazed or ornamented with piped-on decorations. A whole cookie repertoire from one recipe and variations!

Any good general cookbook will give you several recipes for refrigerator cookies. Here are two special ways to make them prettier.

Pinwheels: Divide vanilla-flavored refrigerator cookie dough into two parts. Into one part blend 1 melted (1-ounce) square of chocolate. On a lightly floured board or waxed paper, pat out the light and dark doughs separately into rectangles about ⅛ inch thick. Place the dark dough on top of the light dough; roll them up together firmly, jelly-roll fashion. Refrigerate the roll until chilled; slice and bake.

Checkerboards: Divide the dough and add chocolate to half of it, as above. Then divide both the white and the chocolate doughs in half. Form each of the resulting four pieces of dough into a roll about ½ inch in diameter. Lay one dark roll and one light roll side by side on a lightly floured board or waxed paper; flatten them. Place the second dark roll on top of the bottom light roll, the second light roll on top of the bottom dark roll. Flatten and press all four rolls firmly together. Refrigerate the roll until chilled; slice and bake.

The learn-while-you-eat game
Rolled cookies, in a wide variety of flavors, are old-fashioned favorites. If you make them often, invest in a few cutters of different shapes—there is an almost infinite variety on the market. The shapes of many of these are so attractive that they are decoration in themselves, or the shapes can guide such decoration as piped borders, glaze painting, or combinations of additions and frosting, such as pink-frosted ears and nose for

a rabbit, a splash of white frosting for a cottony tail, raisins or small candies for the eyes.

Decorated animal-shaped cookies make a great hit with children. At a child's birthday party, you might make a giant-size animal cookie, appropriately decorated, for each guest. Pipe the child's name on in decorator's icing and set the animals around the refreshment table to serve as place-cards.

Cutters to use for rolled cookies can be purchased in sets of numbers, including a plus sign and a minus sign, and sets of letters of the alphabet. These offer a dual advantage—besides providing good and simple homemade sweets, cookies made with such cutters are a painless way to teach a young child the alphabet, the spelling of simple words, counting, and simple arithmetic. Number and alphabet cookies can be left as they come from the oven or can be glaze-painted, frosted, or given piped-outline edges for more fun and better taste. Make a big batch—cookies that have spelled out *cat* a dozen times on the living room rug aren't the most sanitary for eating.

Decorating cookies of any shape can be a fun project for children. Supply them with tubes of commercial decorator's frostings and gels, colored sugars, nuts, candies, and raisins and let their talents take over. In fact, a cookie-making party is a very satisfactory method of entertaining young guests and a fine way to pass a rainy Saturday when the picnic or beach trip has had to be postponed.

Cutout cookies, in fancy shapes, can be painted with a tinted egg-yolk wash before they are baked. From the same batch of cookies, choose some to be decorated with "jewels" of colored sugar, using the white of the egg as a base.

Painted cookies: Using a fork, blend 1 egg yolk with ¼ teaspoon of water. Divide it into small portions and tint each portion with food coloring, as desired. Using an artist's brush—a separate one for each color—paint the cookies in colors and designs appropriate to their shapes. You'll get a better effect if you use the paint as an accent, rather than covering the whole cookie.

Jewel cookies: Beat 1 egg white slightly. Set out individual dishes of various colors of sugar, with an after-dinner coffee spoon or a ¼-teaspoon measuring spoon in each. Dip the artist's brush into the egg white and paint the cookies with appropriate designs. Then, using the small spoon, sprinkle colored sugar on the painted portions, brushing it off the unpainted parts.

Giant cookies, decorated as above, or with decorator's frosting piped on, make pretty party favors. Very large cookie cutters are available, or if you have a theme in mind for which you can't find an appropriate cutter, make a pattern out of heavy cardboard, lay the cardboard on the rolled-out cookie dough, and cut around it with a sharp knife.

Cookie glaze: Blend ¾ cup of sifted confectioners sugar with 3 to 4 teaspoons of water and, if desired, a drop or two of food coloring.

Decorator's frosting for cookies: Sift 1 (1-pound) package of confectioners sugar; then sift it again into a medium-size bowl with ½ teaspoon of cream of tartar. Add 3 unbeaten egg whites and ½ teaspoon of vanilla extract. Combine the ingredients with the mixer on low speed. Turn the mixer to medium speed and beat the frosting for about 6 to 8 minutes, until it is so stiff that a knife drawn through it leaves a clean-cut path. Tint the frosting, if desired, and use it with a bag or a cone and tube.

Party-table cookies

Since virtually no one serves afternoon tea any more, you'll have to reserve these for some other company-coming occasion, or make a batch for the family as a treat. The only really bad thing about cookies is that no matter how many you make, it's never quite enough.

Buttery rich within, tastefully (and tastily) decorated, these are cookies that everybody loves to look at, to exclaim over—and then to fall on and demolish as if trying to set a record. Try any one of these or, if you're having a party, a batch of each of three or four kinds. Fortunately, they keep well and thus can be made in advance. Some can be decorated in advance, too; with others, it is best to decorate shortly before serving.

NEEDLEPOINT SHORTBREAD   about 2½ dozen

2 cups sifted all-purpose flour	1 cup butter, softened
¼ teaspoon baking powder	½ cup confectioners sugar
¼ teaspoon salt	

Sift together flour, baking powder, and salt. Combine butter and sugar; beat until creamy. Add flour mixture; blend well. Refrigerate dough 1 hour. Preheat oven to 350°F. On a lightly floured board, pat out dough by hand to a ¼-inch thickness. Using a knife, cut it into diamond shapes. Place cookies 1 inch apart on an ungreased baking sheet. Dip food picks, a separate one for each color, into undiluted liquid food coloring and prick a design into each cookie—dotted edge, scroll, crosshatch, zigzag, or a shaped pattern, such as a bell, a leaf, or so on. Bake 20 to 25 minutes, until firm but not browned.

CORNUCOPIAS   about 5 dozen

¾ cup egg whites (5 to 6)	¼ cup melted shortening, cooled to lukewarm
1⅔ cups sugar	
¼ teaspoon salt	1 cup sifted all-purpose flour
¾ cup melted butter or margarine, cooled to lukewarm	¾ cup finely chopped blanched almonds

Preheat oven to 350°F. Combine unbeaten egg whites with sugar and salt, stirring until sugar is dissolved and mixture is thick. Add butter and shortening; mix well. Stir in flour and almonds until well blended. Drop by scant teaspoonfuls 5 inches apart onto ungreased baking sheet. Bake—no more than 6 at a time—8 to 10 minutes, or until lightly browned at the edges. Let stand ½ minute. Remove cookies from baking sheet and immediately roll around the handle of a wooden spoon to form cone shapes. If cookies harden before you can roll them, return them to the oven for a minute or two. Shortly before serving, fill cornucopias with chocolate butter-cream frosting, using a bag or cone with a plain tube. Dip the ends of frosting in finely chopped pistachio nuts, if desired.

PECAN LACE   3 dozen

¼ cup butter or margarine,
   softened
½ cup firmly packed brown sugar
1 egg

¼ cup finely chopped pecans
2 tablespoons all-purpose flour
¼ teaspoon salt

Preheat oven to 300°F. In a medium-size bowl, cream butter and sugar together until fluffy. Add egg; beat to combine. Stir in pecans, flour, and salt. Drop by half-teaspoonfuls onto lightly greased baking sheet; spread each into a very thin round, 2½ inches in diameter. Make only 2 at a time. Bake 10 minutes, or until golden brown. Cool 1 minute, or until just firm enough to hold shape. Cut in half with a sharp knife. Quickly roll each half into a little cone. Place on a rack to cool and crisp. If cookies become too brittle to shape, return to oven for 30 seconds.

These crisp, nutty little cookies are fine to serve as they are or with a tiny squirt of whipped cream in their centers. Use them, too, to decorate cakes—press them lightly into the top or sides of a layer or tube cake to form a border, or use a single cone to top each serving of a square or rectangular cake.

TWO-TONE BUTTER THINS   about 4½ dozen

1 cup butter or margarine, softened
⅓ cup confectioners sugar
½ teaspoon salt
2 teaspoons vanilla extract

2 cups sifted all-purpose flour
2 teaspoons baking powder
Chocolate Glaze (recipe follows)

In a bowl, cream butter and sugar together; stir in salt and vanilla. Sift together flour and baking powder; add to butter mixture and stir until well blended. Refrigerate dough until you can handle it easily, about 2 hours. Preheat oven to 350°F. Using your fingers, shape dough into 1-inch balls; place on ungreased baking sheet. Using a fork dipped in flour, press balls flat. Bake until golden, 12 to 15 minutes. Cool on racks, bottom sides up. Spread with cookie glaze (see Index). Drizzle parallel lines of Chocolate Glaze across each cookie. With a food pick, draw across lines of chocolate to make a wavy black-and-white pattern.

CHOCOLATE GLAZE

½ cup semisweet chocolate pieces   *¼ cup white corn syrup*

In top of double boiler, over hot—not boiling—water, melt chocolate pieces and corn syrup with 1 tablespoon water; stir frequently. Remove from heat, cool 5 minutes before using.

Cookiewiches: Sandwich two butter thins, bottom sides together, with any flavor butter-cream frosting. Drizzle cookie glaze or Chocolate Glaze over the tops and sprinkle with chopped nuts, silver dragées, or colored sugar.

Marguerites (see Index) and macaroons (see Index) also add variety to a plate of party cookies. And, once you're into the baking of fancy cookies, an exploration of cookbooks will offer you many more to try.

Patterned, pressed, molded

There are several kinds of devices available for making specialty cookies in a variety of sizes and shapes. Old-fashioned cookie stamps, made of ceramic with a design—fruit, flower, or another attractive pattern—in relief or intaglio on the bottom, are once again being made. Make a cookie such as Butter Thins (opposite) and, instead of flattening the cookie with a fork, use the cookie stamp, which will imprint a design on the face of the cookie.

Also available are springerle rolling pins, which imprint their design as the dough is rolled out, as with anise-flavored German cookies, and speculaas forms, which are used to pattern spicy Dutch specialties. There are also metal forms—so handsome that they ought to be displayed on the wall between uses—for colonial gingerbread cookies. Unlike the simple, pudgy gingerbread men we're more familiar with, these turn out elegantly gowned ladies, be-plumed cavaliers, and soldiers in full-dress uniform. All of these forms can be purchased from shops that sell gourmet cookware and, sometimes, from museum shops that sell replicas of the cooking tools of days gone by. Recipes appropriate for the particular tool are usually included.

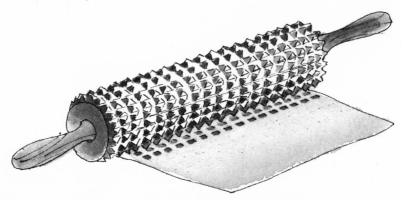

A cookie press is something no dedicated cookie maker should be without. Traditional spritz cookies, and others less traditional but equally delightful, can be made with the press in a great many shapes, then further enhanced with a wide variety of decorations. The press is a metal cylinder with an open bottom. A pattern-making disk is dropped into the bottom, the cylinder is filled with dough, the top (a metal plunger) is screwed in place, and the cookies are pressed directly onto a baking sheet. To change the pattern a different disk is inserted. Be sure to use a recipe designed for spritz or cookie-press cookies and follow it to the letter, because the dough must have the proper consistency. If it's too soft, you'll get nothing but blobs; if it's too stiff, you won't be able to coax the cookies out.

Cookie-press cookies can be decorated with nuts, sprinkles, or colored sugars before baking. Or add chocolate sprinkles or finely grated chocolate to the dough. After baking, they can be frosted or glazed. Ribbon cookies made with the press take on elegance if one end—or both—is dipped in melted semisweet or sweet chocolate, then in chopped pistachios or blanched almonds, silver dragées, or flaked coconut. In whatever form, left plain in their pleasing shapes or decorated, all of these cookies have a buttery, melt-in-your-mouth richness.

Sweet surprises
Filled and wrap-around cookies conceal a bonus of extra flavor and are delightful to look at as well, adding another dimension to cookie making.

Some filled cookies are made up of two rounds or squares with one of many fillings—mincemeat, date–nut, lemon–cheese, for example—sandwiched between and with the edges sealed before baking. Others are larger rounds or squares, with the filling placed on one half of the surface and the dough folded across like a turnover and sealed. A third sort is made after the manner of ravioli. Dabs of filling are spaced at regular intervals on a layer of dough; a second layer of dough is placed on top; then individual cookies are made by cutting between the bits of filling with a fluted pastry wheel, which not only separates the cookies but seals the edges.

Wrap-around cookies are made by rolling a stiffish dough into a ball around some sweet or savory morsel—a milk-chocolate kiss, a coffee-bean candy, a nutmeat, a piece of candied ginger, a little lemon drop—that comes as a happy surprise when the cookie is eaten. One of the many variations on this theme is old-fashioned thumbprint cookies.

THUMBPRINT COOKIES   about 3½ dozen

2 cups sifted all-purpose flour	2 eggs, separated
¼ teaspoon salt	1 teaspoon vanilla extract
1 cup butter or margarine, softened	2 cups finely chopped walnuts
½ cup firmly packed brown sugar	Seedless raspberry preserves

Preheat oven to 350°F. Sift together flour and salt; set aside. In a bowl, combine butter, sugar, egg yolks, and vanilla; beat until fluffy. Work in dry ingredients; blend until smooth. Beat egg whites slightly. Pinch off small pieces of dough, roll into balls about 1 inch in diameter between palms of hands. Dip in egg white, roll in chopped nuts. Place about 2 inches apart on ungreased baking sheets. Flatten slightly, then make indentation in the center of each cookie with the thumb. Bake 12 to 15 minutes, or until set. Cool on wire rack. Fill centers with preserves.

Almond macaroon tarts are still another kind of filled cookie that seems to please everyone. Here is an unusual variation, baked in tiny fluted tart tins (or sandbakelser pans), which are obtainable at gourmet cookware stores or by mail from several sources (see Tools of the Trade).

MACADAMIA MORSELS   about 2 dozen

6 tablespoons butter or margarine, softened	⅔ cup macadamia nuts, finely ground
3 tablespoons sugar	¾ cup sifted confectioners sugar
2 eggs, separated	½ teaspoon vanilla extract
1 cup sifted all-purpose flour	

Cream butter and sugar together until light and fluffy. Add egg yolks and flour; blend until smooth. Refrigerate 1 hour. In a small bowl, combine nuts, confectioners sugar, egg whites, and vanilla. Beat until fluffy. Preheat oven to 350°F. Place chilled dough on a lightly floured board; shape into a roll. With fingers, pinch off small pieces of dough and, with floured hands, pat into lightly buttered tiny tart pans. Fill each three-quarters full with nut mixture. Place on baking sheet. Roll out remaining dough on well-floured board. Cut out shapes, using a tiny cookie or canapé cutter. Place on top of filling. Bake 25 minutes, or until golden. Cool in pans, then remove carefully.

They aren't always baked
Perhaps the prettiest of all cookies are rosettes, which are deep-fat fried. Actually pastries, but serving a cookie purpose, they are delicate in both

flavor and texture, and although they look difficult to make, they are actually relatively easy. You'll need a rosette iron—a handle with one or two prongs to which individual rosette forms can be interchangeably attached. The forms come in a variety of shapes, all of them very pretty, including one that makes a small container into which a little of any savory or sweet mixture can be spooned. Rosettes to be used as cookies need only a dusting of confectioners sugar before serving—they're too pretty and too delicate to be frosted or decorated in any other way. Recipes for rosettes come with the rosette iron, which can be bought in housewares departments or ordered by mail. Nothing's difficult about making these fragile beauties other than learning not to dip the iron into the batter too deeply—if you do, the rosette cooks onto the iron and has to be broken away.

Sweets in little packages
Cookies and their various relatives are easier to make, less chancy, easier to decorate, and easier to store, pack, and carry than cakes. If you're not much of a dessert maker, cookies can be a great starting point for you. And everybody loves the good little mouthfuls. Who ever heard anyone say, "No, thanks—I don't like cookies"?

Decorating Pies

Our grandmothers—at least the good-cook grandmothers of song and story—couldn't be more highly complimented than to be told, "Emma, you certainly do have a light hand with pastry!"

If you want to be known for your good pies, you'll need the same attribute. Pie crust can't stand being slapped around. A good eye is a help too—measure accurately, for the proportions of flour to shortening to water really matter here, down to the last teaspoonful, the last drop.

The best thing about a pie, as with any food, is its flavor. But close on the heels of flavor comes appearance. A pie should be plump and shapely, showing that its cook thought enough of it to devote an extra few moments to fashioning a handsome rim for the crust, a pretty design for the top; that she baked it carefully so that it would be gloriously golden—neither pale and languid-looking nor dark-to-burned brown.

Of course, all pie crusts aren't pastry, and many of these no-pastry (sometimes also no-bake) crusts are a fine starting point for a beginning pie maker. Such crusts can be made of cookie crumbs (chocolate, vanilla, lemon, gingersnap) or graham cracker or cornflake crumbs and/or chopped nuts or coconut. Or a crust can be tender, almost-floats meringue for the angel pies that are such good company desserts because they must be made ahead and given at least twelve hours to mellow. Some crusts are made of pâte à chou (cream-puff pastry) or, simply, of ladyfingers.

Handle with care

For a lovely, like-mother-used-to-make pie, be at all times gentle and easygoing. Roll the pastry lightly, coaxing it into shape rather than bullying it. Drape the crust over your rolling pin and ease it into the pie plate; fit it into place without stretching it. Trim off the overhang with a sharp knife or kitchen scissors, leaving about 1 inch of pastry beyond the edge of the pie plate. Pour or spoon in the filling.

If your pie is to have a top crust, treat it with the same loving care as you roll it. Cut vents in it (in a pattern, not haphazardly) for steam to escape, fold it in half, and ease it over the filling.

About those steam vents: V-shaped cuts, made with a knife, will do—even just poking holes with the tip of the knife will let the steam escape. But you'll have a prettier top crust if you cut the vents with a small cookie or canapé cutter in an evenly spaced pattern. Or use the homey, farm-style trick of cutting steam vents in the shape of a letter of the alphabet—a big A for apple, B for blueberry, L for lemon (the two-crust kind made with sliced lemons), P for rhubarb (no, that's not a mistake; rhubarb was once called pieplant and still is on many midwestern farms), R for raspberry, and so on.

The pie maker's fancy—top crusts

It is not necessarily so that a pie's top crust must be a smooth expanse of pastry with a steam vent here and there. With a little know-how, you can produce a decorative crust that is a thing of beauty, gustatorially speaking. Dress up a top crust a little or a lot, depending on the kind of pie, the time at your disposal, and your artistic leanings. All of the following are pre-baking decorations.

Jewel top: Using your fingers, moisten the top crust—after it is in place—

with a little water. Sprinkle it evenly with sugar. If you're feeling festive, use colored sugar in a color compatible with the filling.

Egg-wash top: Beat together 1 whole egg and 1 tablespoon of milk, or 1 egg yolk and 2 teaspoons of milk or cream. Using a pastry brush, paint over the top crust. If anyone asks you, this is dorure, the easy egg-wash French chefs use to give their pastries a richly golden glaze.

Glimmer top: Cream, undiluted evaporated milk, even plain milk, brushed over a top crust will take away the curse of dullness. So will melted butter or margarine or shortening, or salad oil. Brush it on gently and not too liberally. Then sprinkle the top with sugar if you wish.

Cookie top: Roll out the top crust. While it is still on the board, cut it into shapes with a cookie cutter—round (plain or fluted edge), diamond shaped, bell shaped, whatever. Lay the shapes over the filling in a pleasant pattern, letting them overlap slightly. Pastry shapes made with animal cookie cutters please the children.

Doughnut top: Roll out as above, and cut with a doughnut cutter. Overlap the pastry doughnuts in concentric circles, use the leftover "holes" to decorate the edge of the pie crust.

Strip top I: Roll out as above, and cut the pastry in ½-inch strips with a small, sharp knife or with a fluted pastry wheel. Lay one strip across the top of the pie, then a second at right angles to it, lightly moistening the point where they meet with cold water. Continue to add strips, moistening the center each time, until you have a pattern of wheel spokes.

Strip top II: Roll out and cut the pastry as above. Put the first two strips in place as above. Fold a strip into a wedge shape and position it on one quarter of the pie, leaving a ½-inch space on each side between it and the cross strips. Repeat with three more strips. Then form smaller wedges and place within the first four, again allowing about ½ inch of space on each side.

Spiral top: Roll out and cut the pastry as above. Piece the strips together at the ends to make one long, continuous strip. Moisten the joints with cold water so that they adhere. Work slowly and gently—if you've made a good crust, it's also a delicate one. Twist one end of the strip and put it in place in the center of the pie. Twisting as you go, work the strip out from the center, going round and round to form a spiral.

Lattice top I: Roll out the pastry and cut it into ½-inch strips with a knife or fluted pastry wheel. Lay half the strips over the filling, spaced about 1 inch apart. Lay the remaining strips at right angles to the first set of strips, forming a square or diamond lattice pattern. Result, an unwoven lattice top.

Lattice top II: As directed above, lay half the strips evenly over the filling. Fold every other strip halfway back on itself. Place a cross strip over the center of the pie at right angles to the original strips. Bring the folded strips back over it. Fold back the alternate strips, and place another cross

strip on the pie. Continue until one side of the pie is complete, alternating folded-back strips each time a cross strip is added, then repeat, starting from the center, for the other side of the pie. Result, a woven lattice top.

Cluster top: Roll out the pastry and, using a thimble or a small, round canapé cutter, cut out 36 tiny rounds. Also cut a strip ¼ inch wide and 3 inches long, and two leaf shapes, each about 3 inches at the widest part (for these, try for a grape-leaf shape, cutting freehand or using a cardboard pattern or, if you have it, a real grape leaf as a guide). Starting about ⅓ of the way from one edge, arrange 8 tiny rounds in a row. Just below, starting between two rounds, make a row of 7, then a row of 6, and so on, until you finish at the bottom with a lone round. Arrange the stem (strip of pastry) and leaves at the top of this "bunch of grapes." A very pretty top, not surprisingly, for a concord grape pie.

In making all of these cutout pastry tops, moisten all contact points—where the shapes or strips meet, as well as where they touch the edge of the bottom crust—with cold water. Before the pie goes into the oven, cut off all overhanging pieces of top crust. Bring the overhanging edge of the bottom crust up over the rim of the pie plate and form a decorative edge of any kind you like. If you wish, your fancy top may be painted with milk or cream or egg-wash or with butter or shortening before baking.

To decorate a plain-top two-crust pie after baking, try one of the following glazes.

Lemon glaze: Combine ¾ cup of sifted confectioners sugar with enough lemon juice so that the mixture will pour slowly off a spoon. Dribble the glaze lightly over the cooled top crust of an apple or berry pie.

Chocolate glaze: Melt ½ cup of semisweet chocolate pieces with 1 teaspoon of white corn syrup. Dribble the glaze over the cooled top crust of a peach or pear pie.

Vanilla glaze: Combine ¾ cup of sifted confectioners sugar and ¼ teaspoon of vanilla extract with enough milk so that the mixture will pour slowly off a spoon. Dribble the glaze lightly over the cooled top crust of a mincemeat, cranberry or other berry, or apple pie.

These glazes may be further ornamented, before they set, with chopped nuts, whole nutmeats, grated chocolate, or colored sugars.

The pie maker's fancy—decorative edges

Grandma, that light hand with pastry, prided herself on the various decorative edges with which she ornamented her pies. You can do likewise if you follow these suggestions. (The instructions are for one-crust pies, but all can be adapted for two-crust pies, although for some two-crust pies, extra pastry may be required. All the instructions presuppose that you have fitted the bottom crust in place.)

Fluted rim: Fold the overhanging edge of the pastry under so that it stands up even with the edge of the pie plate. Put the forefinger of one hand on the inside rim of the crust, and the thumb and forefinger of the other hand on the outside at the same point. Pinch the pastry. Move on and repeat all around the pie. For sharper points, pinch each one a second time.

Penny rim: Trim the pastry even with the edge of the pie plate. Using the pastry trimmings and a thimble for a cutter, cut small rounds—you'll need about 48 for a 9-inch pie shell. Moisten the rim of the pie with water and on it place the "pennies," overlapping them slightly, all around the pie. Press them gently to fasten them in place.

Scalloped rim: Fold the overhanging pastry under to make a stand-up edge. Gently press the bowl of a measuring teaspoon on the inside of the rim; with your thumb and forefinger on the outside at the same spot, shape the pastry around the end of the spoon. Repeat all around the pie.

Double-scallop rim: Trim the pastry even with the edge of the pie plate. Using a teaspoon or after-dinner coffee spoon and working from the outside toward the center, gently press a series of scallops into the pastry with the tip of the spoon. Go once around the pie, then go around a second time, pressing the second set of scallops between the first set and in the opposite direction so that they reach to the edge of the plate.

Braided rim: For this you'll need extra pastry—a double-crust recipe for a single-crust pie, a recipe and a half for a double-crust pie. Trim the bottom pastry even with the edge of the pie plate. Roll out the extra pastry and cut it into ¼-inch-wide strips. Braid three of these strips; fasten additional strips to the ends of first three with cold water, and continue to braid. Repeat until you have a braided strip long enough to encircle the pie. Moisten the rim with water and put the braid in place; join the ends neatly and press the braid gently to fasten it in place.

Fork-tine rim: Fold the overhanging pastry under, even with the edge of the pie plate. Gently press it flat. Press the tines of a fork into the pastry—working from the inside—evenly all around the edge. Or press, skip a space the width of the fork, and press again; repeat all around the edge of the pie.

Zigzag rim: Trim the overhanging pastry neatly so that it extends 1½ to 2 inches all around. Using scissors, cut the overhang into a sawtooth pattern. Fold the sawtooth edge toward the center, lapping it over the filling. If you like, make a corresponding pattern in the center on top of the filling with the triangular-shaped leftover pieces of pastry.

Rope rim: Fold the overhanging pastry under to make a stand-up edge. Press a pencil or a wooden skewer into the rim on a slant, twisting slightly as you press, all around the rim of the pie.

Fancy rim: Trim the pastry even with the edge of the pie plate. At intervals around the edge, firmly press any decorative object—a seal, the top of a key, the face of a button—into the pastry.

Opposite: Pies and tarts with fancy tops and edges

Top crust stand-ins

When the pie has no top crust, it's going to look rather undressed unless you do something to decorate it. Here are some of the things you can do.

Crumb and streusel toppings—generally a part of the recipe—are pretty as they are, but even prettier when given a light sprinkling of sifted confectioners sugar after baking. Make an allover drift or outline a pattern, such as a cardboard star, that you place on the top of the pie before you begin to sift.

Lemon pies and various cream pies—vanilla, chocolate, butterscotch—take nicely to meringue. Cautionary note: When making meringue, be sure that you add the sugar called for a little at a time, and that you beat the meringue until all the sugar is dissolved. When you spread the meringue, make certain that it touches the edges of the pie crust all around the outside rim; if not, it will pull away and leave gap-tooth holes. Watch the meringue as it bakes. A light, golden tipping is what you want, and meringue scorches easily if left a moment too long. Instead of piling and spreading the meringue, you can pipe it on with a pastry bag and tube for a pretty, professional-looking topping.

Marshmallows double for meringue on occasion. Place them on top of the filling in a solid covering or in a spiral or in a crosshatch pattern. Place the pie in a hot oven and, as with meringue, keep your eyes open; marshmallows, too, scorch easily. They also melt and make a mess if you're not alert. Just a softened texture and a pretty golden brown are the desired effect.

Whipped cream, plain or sweetened and flavored, is a traditional topping for single-crust pies, no less good to eat and to look at because it's so often used. Pile it high, swirl it on, and add to its goodness with slivered toasted almonds, chopped pistachios or walnuts or pecans, plain (tinted if you like) or toasted coconut, or grated chocolate or chocolate curls (see Index). Sometimes crushed candy is just right—for instance, a chocolate cream pie, topped with whipped cream sprinkled with crushed red-and-white peppermint-stick candy, can be a dish to dream about.

When you make a crumb crust, prepare a generous portion of the crumb mixture and save some of it to sprinkle over the pie's filling or its whipped-cream topping, scattering it at random or in a catch-the-eye pattern of concentric circles, crosshatching, alternating wedges, or how-ever you like. Add nuts, whole or chopped, if they seem called for.

The cheese stands alone

Pie without cheese, the old saw admonishes us, is like a kiss without a squeeze. Perhaps neither ept nor apt, but true, certainly, of most fruit and berry pies. Mincemeat likes cheese, too, and so does pumpkin. A mild cheese cuts what some people consider the too-sweetness of pecan pie.

As for apple pie, in any of its forms, there really should be a law against serving it without cheese. Dedicated turophiles make their apple pies with cheese pastry; rabid ones do so and serve cheese on the side, as well.

CHEESE PASTRY one 9-inch, 2-crust pie

2 cups sifted all-purpose flour
¾ teaspoon salt
1 cup shredded cheddar cheese

⅔ cup shortening
½ cup (or less) ice water

Sift flour and salt together into a medium-size bowl. Add cheese and mix lightly. Add shortening and cut in with a pastry blender or two knives until mixture resembles cornmeal. Sprinkle water evenly over surface. Stir with a fork until all dry particles are moistened and pastry clings together. Roll, fill, and bake as pie recipe directs.

A cream-cheese topping is just right with blueberry, boysenberry, or rhubarb pie. If it incorporates candied ginger, it commands new respect.

GINGERED-CHEESE TOPPING about 1⅓ cups

2 (3-ounce) packages cream
cheese, softened
1 cup confectioners sugar

5 tablespoons light cream
2 tablespoons finely chopped
candied ginger

Beat cream cheese until fluffy. Gradually add sugar, beating after each addition. Add cream; beat until smooth. Gently stir in ginger. Spoon onto pie.

Incomparable with the holiday pies—mincemeat and pumpkin particularly, but also pecan and apple—is a cheese–nut topping made with edam cheese and served in the red cheese shell.

EDAM–PECAN TOPPER about 2½ cups

1 (1-pound) edam cheese
¼ cup coarsely chopped pecans

1 cup light cream
Pecan halves

Soften cheese to room temperature. Cut a thin slice from the top. Hollow out the cheese, leaving a ¼-inch shell of cheese and wax coating. Reserve the shell. Crumble the cheese into a medium-size bowl and add pecans. Pour the cream over and beat until fluffy. Spoon the cheese lightly into the shell and encircle the top with pecan halves.

This rich cheese sauce is just right for a fresh cherry pie with a pretty lattice topping.
Cheddar sauce for pie: In the top of a double boiler, place 6 ounces of cut-

up process sharp cheddar cheese. Add ½ cup of milk. Cook, stirring frequently, over simmering water until the cheese is melted and the mixture is smooth.

Small apple shapes made of yellow cheese are a look-good, taste-good garnish for any fruit or berry pie. They're good with pumpkin and mince pies, too.

Little cheddar apples: Moisten shredded sharp cheddar cheese with just enough light cream so that the cheese will hold a shape. Roll into balls between the palms of the hands. Flatten each ball slightly. Insert a whole clove into one end, a small piece of angelica into the other. Dip one cheek of each apple into paprika for a rosy glow.

Same pies, different tastes

Cheese with pie is great—but suppose you don't like cheese (a pity) or are tired of cheese (unlikely, but possible)? Then try a different sauce, a topper of another flavor. One of these may just fill the bill.

LEMON SAUCE   about 2 cups

1 cup sugar	¼ cup butter or margarine
3 tablespoons cornstarch	3 tablespoons lemon juice
¼ teaspoon salt	2 teaspoons grated lemon peel

In a saucepan, combine sugar, cornstarch, and salt. Gradually add 2 cups boiling water, stirring constantly. Bring to a boil, continuing to stir. Reduce heat and simmer 5 minutes. Remove from heat and blend in butter and lemon juice and peel. Serve at once, or reheat.

Lemon–brandy sauce: Follow the lemon sauce recipe, reducing the lemon juice to 1 tablespoon and adding 3 tablespoons of brandy.

The lemon sauce is very good on apple or other fruit and berry pies. With brandy, it becomes old-fashioned "soft sauce" that once was served as an alternate for or a complement to hard sauce for mince pies. Fine for raisin and apple pies, too.

Brandy hard sauce: Cream together ⅔ cup of butter and 1 cup of confectioners sugar. Gradually add 1 more cup of confectioners sugar, creaming the mixture until it is fluffy. Add ¼ cup of brandy and, if necessary, a little more confectioners sugar for a fluffy consistency. Refrigerate the sauce at least 2 hours before serving.

For any pie that should be, or can be, served warm—mince, apple, raisin, rhubarb, cherry are some—try this delicious and very pretty topper.

ALMOND HARD SAUCE   about 1½ cups

⅔ cup butter	2 tablespoons light cream

½ teaspoon almond extract	½ cup finely chopped blanched
2 cups confectioners sugar	almonds
⅛ teaspoon salt	

Cream butter and almond extract together until softened. Gradually add confectioners sugar and salt, creaming mixture until fluffy. Beat in cream. Blend in almonds. Press the sauce evenly into an 8-inch-square pan, making a layer about ½ inch thick. Refrigerate until firm. With a cookie cutter or knife, cut the sauce into fancy shapes. Serve very cold on hot pie.

The next time you make a creamy-textured pie to serve cold—vanilla, coconut, lemon, or banana cream, or a cheese or an ice cream pie—omit the usual meringue or cream topping and substitute one of these to add new looks and flavor.

CURRANT–RASPBERRY SAUCE about 1½ cups

⅓ cup sugar	½ cup currant jelly
1 teaspoon cornstarch	½ teaspoon vanilla extract
⅛ teaspoon salt	1 tablespoon butter
1 cup fresh red raspberries	

In a saucepan, combine sugar, cornstarch, and salt. Mash raspberries and add to sugar mixture. Add jelly. Bring to a boil over medium heat, stirring constantly. Reduce heat. Cover and simmer 3 minutes. Remove from heat and stir in vanilla and butter. Strain; cool before serving.

CHOCOLATE/ORANGE SAUCE about 1½ cups

½ cup sugar	1 tablespoon butter
⅓ cup instant nonfat dry milk	2 tablespoons orange juice
1 tablespoon cornstarch	1 teaspoon grated orange peel
⅛ teaspoon salt	
1 ounce (1 square) unsweetened chocolate, melted and cooled	

In the top of a double boiler, thoroughly mix sugar, dry milk, cornstarch, and salt. Gradually add 1 cup water, stirring until smooth. Blend in melted chocolate. Bring to a boil over direct heat, stirring constantly. Reduce heat and cook, stirring, 3 minutes. Place over simmering water and cook, covered, 5 minutes. Remove from heat; blend in butter and orange juice and peel. Cool and refrigerate. Serve cold.

MARASCHINO SAUCE about 1⅓ cups

| 1 (8-ounce) jar red maraschino cherries | ½ cup currant jelly |
| 1½ teaspoons cornstarch | 1 tablespoon lemon juice |

Drain cherries, reserving syrup. Measure ⅓ cup cherries; reserve. Halve remaining cherries. To reserved syrup, add water to make ½ cup liquid; place in container of blender and add the ⅓ cup cherries. Blend at medium speed until cherries are puréed, about 30 seconds. Pour into a small saucepan; blend in cornstarch. Add jelly. Cook over medium heat, stirring constantly, until jelly melts and mixture comes to a boil; boil 1 minute. Stir in halved cherries and lemon juice. Refrigerate; serve cold.

To raise a plain vanilla cream pie or a cheese pie to new heights, top it with this easy-do caramel sauce. It's great on ice cream, too.
Caramel sauce: In the top of a double boiler, over simmering water, heat ½ pound of vanilla caramels with ⅓ cup of milk until the caramels are melted and the mixture is smooth.

The prudent pie planner
If you have freezer space, allot some of it to frozen pie shells, purchased or homemade. They can be baked without thawing in a short time, are ready to be filled with any cooked mixture or with ice cream in any number of flavors. They can then be topped with a sauce or with whipped cream or, as a grand gesture, with both.

When you make a single-crust pie, take the extra moment or two to roll out the second half of a two-crust recipe. Fit it into a disposable pie plate and freeze it, or freeze it flat to use as the top crust for some future pie. Or, if you wish, use your cookie or canapé cutters to cut attractive shapes from the extra crust and freeze them for later use as pie decorations. Of course, if there are lurking snackers, they'll be overjoyed to see you spread the rolled-out second crust with a little soft butter, cinnamon, and sugar, or with marmalade and chopped walnuts. Roll it up and slice it jelly-roll fashion; bake the pastries along with your pie shell for instant no-trouble treats.

Round is not the only shape
No ukase has been handed down directing that all pies must be circular. If you're feeding a crowd, make a pie in a rectangular pan. Cut it into squares or, if you feel the eaters won't recognize pie unless it's pie shaped, cut it on the diagonal in one direction, then cut across the slanted lines—you'll produce pie-shaped wedges after all.

For a change from big round pies, make little ones—tarts. Individual tart pans, about 3 inches in diameter, are available fluted or plain. Square tart pans are available, too. Or, if you're thrifty, shape the pie crusts over the bottoms of muffin tins, pinching them into shape.

Turnovers, triangular or semicircular, make a nice change, too. Any two-crust pie recipe can be used to make turnovers of either shape. Roll out the pastry, half at a time, and cut it into 4-inch squares or 5- or 6-inch rounds (use a giant cookie cutter or trace around a saucer). Place about a tablespoon of filling on one half, fold the other half over, seal the edges, and prick the tops in several places with a fork to allow steam to escape. Two cautions: Don't use too much filling and make certain the edges are well sealed or you'll have leakage problems.

Tiny turnovers, made with 2½-inch squares or 3-inch rounds of pastry, are pretty, too. Serve them as you would cookies, along with a dish of ice cream—a pleasant switch on pie à la mode. Fill them with a small dab of thick applesauce (spiced or not) or a little mincemeat or with thick preserves of any flavor. If you like, add spice to the pastry for turnovers, large or small, or use cheese pastry (see Index). Paint with egg-wash (see Index) for a sparkling shine, or simply sprinkle the tops of plain-pastry turnovers with white or colored sugar or with a mixture of cinnamon and sugar.

Like mother used to make

For some reason, pies invoke nostalgia—much more so than cakes or any other kind of dessert. Men, especially, tend to remember the pies their mothers made—even those mothers who, in reality, could barely boil water.

If you'll bring a little extra effort to the task, you too can make pies that will linger on the palates and in the minds of those who consume them long after the last crumb is gone. There's a great deal of simple satisfaction to be gained from making pies that are not only remembered, but worth remembering.

Decorating Other Desserts

Cakes, pies, cookies—these are the dessert standbys. But there's a wider world, made up of bavarian creams, sweet hot or cold soufflés, cheesecakes, puddings, icebox cakes, spanish creams, custards, trifles, cream puffs and eclairs, ice creams and their like, as well as dozens of fruit desserts and fruit-and-other-sweets combinations. Many of these desserts, particularly the molded ones, are very handsome in themselves, needing only a fluff of whipped cream—spooned or piped through a pastry tube—or a sauce to finish them.

Fruit in its many shapes and colors is beautiful, particularly if you take the time to pick out unblemished pieces for a fruit bowl or tray; nature has provided many fruits with a natural wax that needs only to be buffed with a paper towel to bring up a glimmering shine.

Dessert crepes, prepared and frozen far in advance (they're easy to make; they freeze well and thaw quickly), are like money in the bank when you need a special dessert in a hurry. Crepes suzette are only the beginning of a vast repertoire of dessert crepes. Consult a good general cookbook for crepes recipes and ideas for fillings and sauces. If you have a chafing dish, finish the crepes at the table and flame them for a spectacular conclusion to the meal.

Ice cream in the freezer furnishes another moment's-notice flambéed dessert. Make a hot brandied fruit sauce (canned fruit will work here) in the chafing dish, set it afire and ladle the flaming sauce over ice cream. It's almost as lovely to look at as it is to eat.

Cheese and fruit are sure to please

The easiest of desserts to prepare and warmly welcomed by everyone, fruit with cheese is an unbeatable combination and can be a very handsome one. Choose a good-looking tray or platter, large enough to accommodate several kinds of cheese and several varieties of fruit. If the container you choose is attractive, leave it as it is; if not, line it with flat leaves, such as grape leaves. Arrange the cheese in a pleasing pattern, keeping all of each kind together so that guests won't have to poke around on the tray to find what they want. Pile polished whole fruit or chunks or slices of prepared fruit at one end of the platter or, if you're pressed for space, in a pretty bowl. There should be crackers, too—plain, bland ones that won't fight for supremacy with the fruit and cheese flavors.

Be sure to provide tools—knives, cutters, and scoops for the cheese, butter knives to use as spreaders, and fruit knives if you've left the fruit whole. And, of course, dessert plates.

Bear in mind, in choosing cheese for such a dessert, that tastes differ. If you set out a combination of a whole soft cream cheese, a plump little edam or gouda, slices of swiss, fingers of cheddar, wedges of camembert, triangles of roquefort, and cubes of gjetost or mysost, you'll have something for everyone. Strident cheeses, such as bierkäse or limburger, don't belong here. Save them for a black bread, beer, and cheese party, which is an easy and inexpensive way to entertain.

Offer variety in the fruit, too. Pears and apples are ones that leap to mind, and they're available all year round. But peaches and nectarines, navel oranges and tangerines, grapes of all sorts, fingers of fresh pineapple, bing or royal anne cherries, cubes or wedges of papaya or mango or melon, big whole strawberries or loganberries or boysenberries—all these are good and unusual with cheese. At a time when many fresh fruits are out of season, offer dried fruits or dishes of excellent preserves, such as jam made of whole wild strawberries or jellies such as bar-le-duc or quince or guava.

The epitome of fruit-plus-cheese

Cheesecake with a fruit topping, in many combinations of flavors, makes a hearty, delicious, and lovely-to-look-at ending for a light meal. Find recipes in any good cookbook. Try combinations such as vanilla cheese-cake with cherries, orange with blueberries, lemon with raspberries and mint, chocolate with glazed fresh orange slices. Bring the cheesecake to the table whole, because half the joy of eating lies in seeing the food at its best. Decorate the plate with more of the whole or sectioned fruit and with fresh green leaves for contrast.

Perhaps the most exquisite of fruit/cheese desserts is coeur à la crème. Traditionally, it is prepared in a heart-shaped perforated ceramic or porcelain mold or a basket designed just for this purpose, but you may pack it into a round, deep sieve, if you like, because it comes unmolded to the table. Whatever you use, the mold must be lined with doubled cheesecloth wrung out in cold water and the dessert must be refrigerated overnight.

COEUR A LA CREME

12 to 15 servings

3 (8-ounce) packages cream cheese, at room temperature

2 cups creamed cottage cheese, at room temperature

¼ cup heavy cream

Fresh strawberries, raspberries, or other fresh fruit or preserves

Combine the cheeses with the cream and whirl in the blender (half at a time) or beat at high speed of an electric mixer until smooth. Press lightly into a prepared 2-quart mold, or into two smaller ones; refrigerate overnight. When ready to serve, unmold on a leaf-lined plate; remove cheesecloth gently. Decorate the top and surround the base of the mold with fruit.

Some recipes call for the addition of confectioners sugar and vanilla, but connoisseurs prefer the cheese unsweetened and unflavored. If you wish, provide a bowl of confectioners sugar so that guests may sweeten the fruit if it is too tart for their taste.

Visions of sugarplums

Glacéed strawberries are a beautiful dessert, raising a plain cake or cookies to ambrosial heights. Glacéed or spiced nuts, candied fruit peels (see Index), and crystallized violets and rose petals all dress a chilled dessert, such as a spanish or bavarian cream or a cold soufflé, with incomparable elegance. None of these is difficult to make, and some can be made far in advance, to wait obligingly for their big moment.

Make the glacéed strawberries only when the largest, plumpest, most flavorful berries are in season. Refrigerate them no more than an hour before serving.

GLACEED STRAWBERRIES · 6 to 8 servings

24 *large strawberries*	1 *tablespoon light corn syrup*
2 *cups sugar*	⅛ *teaspoon cream of tartar*

Prepare strawberries (leave the hulls on) by brushing clean with a soft pastry brush—do not wash them. They must be perfect, without soft spots. Place them on paper towels on a tray, and refrigerate. Line a second tray with aluminum foil; set aside. In a heavy 2-quart saucepan, combine sugar and corn syrup with ½ cup water. Bring to a boil over moderate heat, stirring occasionally. Mix cream of tartar with 1 teaspoon water and stir in. Turn heat to high; place a candy thermometer in the saucepan. Let syrup boil, without stirring, to a temperature of 290°F. (hard crack). Remove from heat at once. Raise the leaves of the hull of a cold strawberry to make a handle; holding the berry by this, dip it into the syrup to coat it completely. Work rapidly. Remove strawberry at once and hold over pan so excess glaze drips off. Place on foil. Repeat with remaining berries; refrigerate immediately. If necessary, reheat syrup as you work to maintain a temperature of 290°F.

GLAZED NUTS · about 1½ cups

2 *cups sugar*	*Dash of salt*
⅛ *teaspoon cream of tartar*	1½ *cups nutmeats*

Oil a marble slab or heavy platter; set aside. In a heavy saucepan, combine sugar, cream of tartar, and salt with ⅔ cup water. Bring to a boil, stirring only until sugar is dissolved. Put a candy thermometer in place and continue to cook, without stirring, until syrup reaches 310°F. Remove from heat at once; dip bottom of pan into cold water for a moment to stop cooking. Place pan over hot water to keep syrup from hardening. Drop whole or half nutmeats into syrup, one at a time; remove at once. Turn nuts upside down on slab or platter. They will harden almost at once and are then ready to use.

SPICED NUTS   about 1¾ cups

2 cups sugar	2 teaspoons ground ginger
2 teaspoons salt	1 tablespoon ground cloves
1 teaspoon ground nutmeg	2 egg whites
3 tablespoons ground cinnamon	1¾ cups nutmeats

Combine sugar, salt, and spices; sift together 3 times. Beat egg whites lightly; stir in 2 tablespoons cold water. Place nutmeats in a wire strainer; dip into egg-white mixture until all are well coated. Drain well; roll in sugar mixture. Preheat oven to 200°F. Spread half the sugar mixture in a shallow pan; spread nuts over, separating each one. Cover with remaining sugar mixture. Bake 3 hours. Remove from oven; place nuts in a strainer and sift off excess sugar; it can be stored and reused.

Candied rose petals and whole violets: Choose perfect rose petals. Remove the stems from the violets. Dip each separately into lightly beaten egg white, then into superfine granulated sugar. Lay them separately on a plate liberally sprinkled with the sugar; sprinkle lightly with more sugar. Put in a warm, dry place to dry. Mint leaves (you will need to wash, then completely dry them first) can be candied by the same method.

Crystallized rose petals and whole violets: Choose richly fragrant violets or roses and prepare as above. Place a wire rack in a 10- x 14- x 2-inch pan; set aside. In a large, heavy saucepan, combine 3 pounds of sugar with 1 quart of water; cook to 238°F. on a candy thermometer. Pour a layer of the syrup into the prepared pan deep enough to cover the rack. Allow the syrup to cool. Spread the rose petals or violets on the rack, making certain each is completely covered with syrup. Cover the pan with a wet towel (to prevent the sugar from crystallizing between the flowers) and let it stand for 5 hours. Add more cooled syrup to cover the flowers again. Cover the pan with a wet towel and let it stand overnight. Lift the rack from the pan and set it on a tray or baking sheet so that the flowers can drain and dry.

Any shape, as long as it's chocolate

Many kinds of wonderful-to-look-at, wonderful-to-taste decorations can be made from chocolate—fragile little cones, delicate lifelike leaves, whisper-thin wheels, small fluted cups. The cones, leaves, and wheels can be used to decorate any kind of cold dessert—such as a bavarian cream, a cold soufflé, a custard, an icebox cake—or to add elegance to a dish of ice cream; no law says that they can't be used to ornament the frosting of cakes, big or small, either, or the cream-topped surfaces of pies. As for the cups, they can be filled with any kind of cooked custard or pudding, or with ice cream or sherbert, to turn a plain dessert into a festive one. These chocolate creations require a light, quick touch, considerable patience, and a certain amount of dexterity, but they can be made well ahead of time and refrigerated or frozen until you are ready to use them.

Chocolate cones: Cut waxed paper into six 5-inch squares; cut each square in half to make triangles. Roll each triangle into a cone, making sure that the tip of the cone is tightly closed, so that the chocolate will not leak; tape the cone to secure it. In the top of a small double boiler, over simmering water, melt 6 squares of semisweet chocolate; remove the chocolate from the heat before it is completely melted and stir it smooth. Using a small, pointed paring knife, spread the inside of each cone with the chocolate, making certain to cover the cone completely. Place the cones on a plate in the freezer until the chocolate is set and firm—only a few minutes. Then—be gentle-handed—peel away the waxed paper. Freeze or refrigerate the cones until you are ready to use them. In positioning them on the dessert, handle them as little as possible.

Chocolate leaves: Use fresh, firm green leaves of a pretty shape. Choose those that have well-raised veins on the back side of the leaf. Gardenia leaves work well—so do the leaves of roses or ivy. Leave enough stem on each leaf to serve as a handle. Wash the leaves, pat them completely dry on both sides with a towel, and set them aside. In the top of a small double boiler, over simmering water, melt squares of semisweet chocolate—6 squares will be sufficient to do a dozen small leaves. Remove the chocolate from the heat before it is completely melted and stir it smooth. Hold a leaf by its stem, upside down—that is, with the veined underside of the leaf on top. Using a small metal spatula, spread chocolate thinly and evenly over the leaf, making sure that the chocolate does not run onto the other side of the leaf. With your fingertip, very gently wipe the edges of other side of the leaf to make certain there is no chocolate there. Place the leaves, chocolate side up, on a plate in the refrigerator or freezer until the chocolate is just set and firm. Carefully and slowly peel off each green leaf, starting at the stem end. Handle the chocolate leaves as little as possible. Place them on a plate and refrigerate or freeze them.

Chocolate shapes: In the top of a double boiler, over simmering water, melt 6 ounces of semisweet chocolate squares with 2 tablespoons vegetable shortening. Spread the mixture into a thin sheet on foil; refrigerate it until it is firm. Using canapé cutters, cut out any desired small shapes—playing card pips, stars, crescents, or such. Return them to the refrigerator until you're ready to use them.

Chocolate cups: Place 6 fluted paper baking cups into muffin pans. Melt the chocolate and shortening as for the shapes, above. Drop 1 tablespoon of the chocolate mixture into each paper cup. Refrigerate the chocolate just until it begins to set. With the back of a spoon, push and spread the chocolate to coat the inside of each cup, making certain not to leave empty spaces. Refrigerate the cups until the chocolate is set and firm. Gently peel off the paper cups and return the chocolate to the refrigerator or freeze until you're ready to serve.

Make, freeze, serve

Ice creams and other frozen desserts, like almost everything else you like to serve to family or guests, are at their very best when they're homemade. However, you can look to high-quality readymade materials to help you—the very best hand-packed, natural flavored ice creams, for instance, from which to make a magnificent dessert such as a two-color, double-flavored bombe or a baked alaska.

Ice cream bombe: You will need a mold—one without many intricate convolutions in its pattern is best for this dessert. A mold that has its own cover is most desirable. Refrigerate the mold to chill it well before using. Line it with a ¾-inch layer of slightly softened ice cream, water ice, or sherbet, spreading the layer evenly. Cover the mold (with buttered waxed paper, then with tied-on foil, if the mold does not have its own cover) and place it in the freezer until the layer is frozen solid. Then fill the center with a second kind of ice cream, ice, or sherbet—one that complements both the flavor and the color of the outer layer. Cover the mold again and freeze the bombe until it is firm. To unmold the bombe, dip the mold quickly in hot water, dry it, and invert it on a chilled serving platter. Garnish the bombe quickly with fruit (plain or macerated in brandy or kirsch or a fruit-flavored liqueur) or with piped whipped cream or with a thick sauce (fudge or caramel) that will stiffen on the cold ice cream. To serve it, slice it with a silver knife briefly dipped in hot water.

Here are some fine flavor/color combinations:

> chocolate ice cream, praline ice cream
> orange ice, chocolate ice cream
> vanilla ice cream, apricot ice
> strawberry ice cream, pineapple sherbet
> maple-walnut ice cream, vanilla ice cream
> lemon sherbet, raspberry sherbet
> pistachio ice cream, raspberry sherbet
> coffee ice cream, chocolate chip ice cream
> chocolate-mint ice cream, vanilla ice cream
> lemon ice cream, lime sherbet
> coconut ice cream, caramel ice cream
> peach ice cream, lemon sherbet

With those ideas to get you started, let your imagination and your own flavor preferences guide you. There is, of course, nothing to prevent you from making a three- or even a four-flavor bombe.

On some occasion, turn a bombe into a baked alaska.

Baked alaska: Have ready a bombe frozen in a simple mold, such as a metal mixing bowl. You will also need a layer of sponge or other plain cake at least 1 inch larger than the diameter of the mold, and a meringue made in the proportions of 5 egg whites to ¾ cup of superfine sugar. Preheat the oven to 450°F. Place the cake on an ovenproof serving dish and unmold the bombe on it. Working quickly, frost the bombe with the meringue, making sure that it covers the bombe completely and touches the cake layer all around. Place the alaska in the oven for about 5 minutes, or until the meringue is lightly browned. Watch it constantly. Remove and serve it at once.

Good-quality ice cream in the freezer plus a selection of liqueurs and fruit brandies equal handsome, delicious desserts in virtually no time. Spoon the ice cream into your prettiest dishes, sauce it with a liqueur and, if you like, garnish it with chopped nuts or with fresh or glacéed fruit. Here are some good combinations:

coffee ice cream, crème de cacao
chocolate ice cream, cherry heering
banana ice cream, kahlua or other coffee liqueur
orange ice, green crème de menthe
peach ice cream, amaretto
caramel or butterscotch ice cream, crème de noyaux
lime ice, crème d'ananas
chocolate-almond ice cream, curaçao

If you have crushed praline (see Index) on hand, or a jar of brandied chestnuts or chestnuts in vanilla syrup, you can use these to turn a plain dish of ice cream into an instant culinary triumph. Even maple syrup, plus walnuts or pecans, dresses up a plain dish of ice cream. Remember when serving ice cream combinations that the serving dish counts, too. Don't feel that you must confine yourself to nappies and sherbet glasses —goblets, footed tumblers, parfait glasses, on-the-rocks and other cocktail-type glasses all serve well to hold these desserts attractively.

What's for dessert?

If you answer "pudding," almost all children—almost all husbands, too— will be pleased. Serve even the simplest puddings with imagination and they will be even more welcome.

Try layering plain vanilla or chocolate pudding in parfait or other footed glass dishes with chopped nuts, crushed candies, coconut, fresh fruit or preserves, or chocolate or other sauces. Or make two flavors of simple pudding, such as blancmange, and spoon them into the dishes in alternating layers or swirl them together as you do the batter for marble cake. Or simply change the flavor sometimes—lemon rice pudding instead of vanilla, chocolate bits in the bread pudding instead of raisins, fruit juice substituted for all or part of the milk in tapioca pudding. Or learn a totally different way to present an old favorite, such as this version of rice pudding, which is fit to grace the most elegant of tables.

RASPBERRY RICE CROWN   8 servings

1 cup raw rice
1 tablespoon plus 2 teaspoons
   unflavored gelatin
½ cup sugar
3 cups cold milk
⅛ teaspoon salt

1½ teaspoons vanilla extract
3 cups fresh raspberries or drained
   frozen whole raspberries,
   divided
1½ cups heavy cream, whipped
¾ cup red currant jelly

Cover rice with water; bring to a boil. Cook gently 5 minutes. Drain. Combine gelatin and sugar; stir into milk. Place in the top of a double boiler; heat, stirring, until gelatin and sugar are dissolved. Add drained rice, salt, and vanilla. Cover and cook, over simmering water, until rice is very tender, about 30 minutes, stirring twice during cooking time. Remove from heat; cool to room temperature. Press 1 cup raspberries through a strainer to remove seeds. Fold raspberry purée and whipped cream into rice mixture. Turn into a decorative 1½-quart mold; refrigerate 8 hours or overnight. Shortly before serving, melt jelly over low heat. Cool 10 minutes. Pour over remaining raspberries. Unmold pudding, garnish with glazed raspberries. Serve with additional whipped cream, if desired.

You can ring changes on almost any family favorite. Suppose you want to make that good old standby, upside down cake. No pineapple? Try peaches or apricots or plums. No canned fruit at all? Try prunes or raisins. Or substitute sliced oranges. Or mixed glacéed fruit. No fruit of any kind? Butter the baking dish heavily, sprinkle with brown sugar, a little orange juice—or, in a pinch of pinches, just a little water—and a few chopped nuts.

If you have a freezer, you can always have whipped cream on hand to dress up a simple dessert in a hurry. Whip the cream, put it in a pastry bag fitted with a large drop-flower tube, and drop rosettes of the cream onto a foil-lined baking sheet. Place the sheet in the freezer until the rosettes are firm, then repackage them in a container or bag; they're ready to unthaw and use on a moment's notice.

Dessert is, for most people, the delight of any meal, the part looked forward to with eagerness. No matter what you offer, from the simplest dish of stewed fruit to the most elaborate of concoctions, bring it to the table prettily served and attractively decorated, and nobody will be disappointed.

It's Good Manners
to Eat the Centerpiece

Some foods are, by their nature, show-stoppers. Sumptuous in appearance, tantalizing in taste, they say to your guests that you have labored lovingly to create something very special for them.

The day of the sit-down dinner, other than for a very small group, is gone. Few of us have the room, the equipment—not to mention the servants—that such lavish entertaining requires. If you plan to give a brunch, luncheon, or dinner for more than six, you will probably opt for buffet service. That doesn't mean that you'll want to treat the party as a slapdash affair. A buffet meal should be different from a sit-down one only in kind, not in quality.

In buffet service the food itself provides the major table decoration, much more so than at a sit-down meal. There should be at least one spectacular dish to serve as a focal point—centerpiece—to lend the table grace and a touch of flamboyance. As with every food that is good to look at, the centerpiece must also be good to eat, as unusual and challenging to the palate as to the eye.

"Come for brunch"

A weekend or holiday buffet brunch is a splendid way to entertain and—a bonus—is likely to be much less costly than a dinner for the same number of guests. To serve as the focal point of the buffet table, plan on a pair of handsome and delicious homemade coffee cakes. They can be baked the day before or, if you like, any time up to a month in advance and frozen.

BALKAN COFFEE BRAIDS   2 coffee cakes

4¾ cups (or more) all-purpose flour, divided
2 packages active dry yeast
1¼ cups milk
⅔ cup firmly packed brown sugar
6 tablespoons butter or margarine
1 teaspoon salt
3 eggs, divided

1 teaspoon ground cardamom
1 teaspoon finely shredded lemon peel
1½ cups white raisins
½ cup sliced almonds, divided
⅔ cup sliced candied cherries, divided

In the large bowl of an electric mixer, combine 2½ cups flour and the yeast. In a saucepan, combine milk, sugar, butter, and salt and heat just until warm (115 to 120°F.), stirring constantly so that butter will be almost melted. Add to flour mixture; add 2 eggs and 1 egg white, reserving the third egg yolk. Add cardamom and lemon peel; beat at low speed, scraping sides of bowl constantly, until blended; beat at high speed 3 minutes. By hand, stir in enough remaining flour to make a moderately stiff dough. Stir in raisins. Turn dough out onto a lightly floured board or cloth; knead 6 to 8 minutes, or until dough is smooth and elastic. Shape in a ball; place in a lightly greased bowl, turning dough to grease entire surface. Cover; let rise in a warm place until double in bulk, 1 to 1½ hours. Punch dough down; divide in half. Cover one part of dough and reserve. Divide second part of dough in half; cut one half into thirds. Roll each third into a rope 18 inches long; braid ropes very loosely. Place on greased baking sheet, tucking ends under to seal. Divide remaining part of dough into fourths. Roll 3 of these pieces into ropes 14 inches long; braid as before and place on top of first braid, tucking ends under. Cut remaining piece of dough into thirds, roll each third into a rope 12 inches long; braid as before and place on top of second braid. Beat remaining egg yolk with a few drops of milk; brush braid with half of yolk mixture; sprinkle with half of almonds and half of cherries. Using the reserved dough, repeat to make a second coffee cake; brush with remaining egg yolk, sprinkle with remaining almonds and cherries. Cover both with a towel; let rise until nearly double in bulk, 30 to 45 minutes. Preheat oven to 350°F. Bake 25 to 30 minutes, or until done and nicely browned.

"Come for lunch"

On a summer day, invite a group of friends for a buffet lunch. As the focal point of the meal, offer a magnificent four-layer mousse that you have made the day before. It is one of the most delectable of cold foods, and absolutely beautiful to look at with its decorated aspic top, its alternating layers of color. The recipe looks more complicated than it actually is—the only trick is in having all the ingredients prepared and close at hand before you start assembling the work of art.

DARIA'S SPECIAL MOUSSE   10 to 12 servings

Have ready in advance: 6¼ cups very strong, well-flavored, clarified chicken stock (made at home or from cans); a 4-quart mold (a glass or metal mixing bowl will do beautifully).

aspic layer:

1 tablespoon (envelope) unflavored gelatin	12 pitted ripe olives, sliced
1¼ cups chicken stock, divided	12 sprigs fresh tarragon, washed and well dried

Soften gelatin in ¼ cup stock. Heat remaining stock; add softened gelatin and stir until dissolved. Cool, then refrigerate gelatin until it is the consistency of unbeaten egg white. Pour a very thin layer into bottom of mold. Refrigerate a few minutes, until set. Dip olive rings into remaining stock mixture; position in a circle around edge of mold. Dip tarragon sprigs in stock, position in mold so that they fan out from center to edge. Refrigerate a few minutes, until set. Spoon on remaining stock; refrigerate until set.

ham layer:

1 tablespoon (envelope) unflavored
   gelatin
1¼ cups chicken stock, divided
3 cups cubed cooked ham

1 cup heavy cream
Salt and white pepper
1 tablespoon onion juice

Soften gelatin in ¼ cup stock. Heat remaining stock; add softened gelatin and stir until dissolved. Refrigerate until consistency of unbeaten egg white. Purée ham in blender with gelatin mixture, a part at a time. Whip cream until soft peaks form. Fold into ham mixture. Season with salt and pepper to taste and onion juice. Spoon over set aspic layer in mold, return to refrigerator until set.

herb layer:

1 tablespoon (envelope) unflavored
   gelatin
1¼ cups chicken stock, divided
1¼ cups shredded watercress leaves
1¼ cups finely shredded spinach
   leaves

2 tablespoons finely snipped
   parsley
1 tablespoon finely snipped
   tarragon leaves
1 cup heavy cream

Soften gelatin in ¼ cup stock. Heat remaining stock; add softened gelatin and stir until dissolved. Refrigerate until consistency of unbeaten egg white. Place watercress, spinach, parsley, and tarragon in a bowl; pour on boiling water to cover. Let stand 5 minutes. Drain, spread on paper towels and dry well with more towels. Purée in blender with gelatin mixture. Whip cream until soft peaks form; fold into herb mixture. Spoon over set ham layer; return to refrigerator until set.

tomato layer:

1 tablespoon (envelope) unflavored
   gelatin
1¼ cups chicken stock, divided
1 large onion, finely chopped
3 cups peeled, seeded, and
   chopped tomatoes

Salt and pepper
½ teaspoon sugar
1 teaspoon dried basil
1 cup heavy cream

Soften gelatin in ¼ cup stock. Heat ½ cup stock; add softened gelatin and stir until dissolved. Refrigerate until consistency of unbeaten egg white. In a skillet, combine onion, tomatoes, salt and pepper to taste, sugar, and basil. Add remaining stock. Cook over low heat, stirring often, until onion is completely cooked and tomato is almost reduced to a paste, about 30 minutes. Cool. Purée in blender with gelatin mixture. Whip

Opposite: For lunch—Daria's Special Mousse

168

cream until soft peaks form. Fold into tomato mixture. Spoon over set herb layer; return to refrigerator until set.

chicken layer:

1 tablespoon (envelope) unflavored gelatin	Salt and pepper
1¼ cups chicken stock, divided	¼ teaspoon ground nutmeg
3 cups cubed cooked chicken	½ teaspoon dried thyme
	1 cup heavy cream

Soften gelatin in ¼ cup stock. Heat remaining stock; add softened gelatin and stir until dissolved. Refrigerate until consistency of unbeaten egg white. In blender, purée (a part at a time) chicken, gelatin mixture, salt and pepper to taste, nutmeg, and thyme. Whip cream until soft peaks form. Fold into chicken mixture. Spoon over set tomato layer. Refrigerate overnight.

To finish the dish: unmold on a bed of watercress sprigs; surround with celery rosettes (see Index) and tomato roses (see Index).

"Come for cocktails"

Unless you're informally inviting people to drop over for a drink, a cocktail party requires as much care in planning the food as it does the liquor. Cocktail parties have a way of stretching out and out—never mind that the invitations said five to seven o'clock—and people at cocktail parties like plenty to nibble on, because a good half of them never get any dinner after such a gathering.

What's the focal point of a table of good things to nibble on? Cheese, dressed up to go to the party. Here are two ways with cheese that elevate it far above the put-a-chunk-on-a-cracker category. Neither is a great deal of trouble and both can be made ahead of time.

SHERRY/CHEDDAR/WALNUT WHEEL   24 cocktail servings

1¼ pounds sharp cheddar cheese   *1½ cups chopped walnuts, divided*
¾ cup (about) dry sherry   *Walnut halves*

Shred the cheese, using the largest mesh of your grater. Place in a bowl; moisten with sherry and stir and mash lightly until the cheese is a cohesive mass. Lightly oil a 7-inch springform pan. Press half the cheese mixture into the pan in an even layer. Sprinkle 1 cup chopped walnuts over the cheese and press into place. Top with remaining cheese; press into place. About ¾ hour before serving, remove sides of pan and press remaining chopped nuts into sides of cheese wheel. Garnish top with walnut halves. Surround with crisp wholewheat crackers.

Brie-with-a-braid: In a good general cookbook, find a recipe for a crusty-type white bread, such as french or italian bread. Buy a brie cheese and measure its diameter. Make up the bread dough, following the recipe through the first rising. Punch down the dough, if the recipe directs, and divide it into three pieces. In the center of a large, greased baking sheet, mark a circle the diameter of the brie plus 2 inches. Roll each third of the bread dough into a rope long enough so that, when the ropes are braided, the braid will surround the marked circle on the baking sheet. Braid the dough and place it on the sheet around the circle, joining the ends. Bake the bread according to recipe directions. To serve, place the brie on a round serving platter or tray and slip the bread braid around it. Each person breaks off a piece of the crusty bread and tops it with a piece of brie.

"Come for dinner"
When you'd like to have guests for dinner, but would prefer not to reduce your food budget to a shambles, what leaps to mind? Pasta. Unfortunately, that's what leaps to everyone's mind to the point where the world is filled with diners-out who are up to their armpits in lasagna and linguini with clam sauce.

Turn your thoughts in other directions. What, other than pasta, stretches a small amount of meat and does it deliciously? Vegetables. Eggplant? Yes, of course—moussaka. Peppers? By all means—baked with a savory meat/rice filling. Beans? Surely—a great (but not all that inexpensive) cassoulet. Cabbage? Indeed, wonderful peasanty stuffed cabbage. But not your ordinary, run-of-the-mill stuffed cabbage. Rather, a handsome, curly-leafed savoy with a luscious filling and a wonderful sauce that will turn out to be a thing of beauty on your buffet table and a joy to those lucky enough to be invited to share it.

STUFFED SAVOY CABBAGE

8 to 10 servings

1 (8-ounce) package herb-seasoned
  stuffing mix
1 (4-pound) head savoy cabbage
1 pound pork sausage
¾ cup finely chopped onion
2 cups ground raw chicken or
  turkey
½ cup chopped parsley

2 eggs, lightly beaten
1 teaspoon leaf sage, crumbled
1 teaspoon salt
¼ teaspoon pepper
2 (13¾-ounce) cans chicken
  broth
Mushroom Sauce (recipe follows)

In the blender, reduce the stuffing mix to crumbs; reserve. Line a 12-cup mixing bowl with a triple layer of cheesecloth large enough so that it hangs several inches over the edge; set aside. Using a small, sharp knife, take out the core of the cabbage. One by one, carefully pull off the leaves. Reserve eight of the largest leaves; put the remaining leaves into a large kettle of boiling water; leave in the water until pliable, 3 to 5 minutes. Remove to paper towels to drain well. Place the large reserved leaves into the boiling water for 1 minute; remove and drain; reserve. In a large skillet, cook sausage meat, breaking it up as it cooks, until it is lightly browned and no pink color remains. Add onion; cook until limp but not brown. Add chicken; cook, stirring, until meat turns white, about 5 minutes. (Turkey will take a little longer.) Stir in ⅔ cup water and bring to a boil. Remove from heat, blend in reserved stuffing mix, parsley, eggs, sage, salt, and pepper. (A note on taste: add additional seasonings if you wish—the mixture should be highly seasoned, as the cabbage will absorb much of the flavor.)

Place a double layer of reserved cabbage leaves in the cheesecloth-lined bowl, overlapping them slightly and letting the tops hang a little over the side of the bowl. Place one-third of pork–chicken mixture in the bowl, cover with cabbage leaves; repeat the layering twice more, ending with cabbage. Fold the overhanging leaves over the top, gather the cheesecloth tightly, and press the stuffed cabbage into a ball shape; tie securely with string. (At this point you may refrigerate it and cook it later, if you like.) Place the cabbage in a deep saucepan into which it fits without much space around it. Add chicken broth; bring to a boil. Cover tightly; lower heat and simmer gently 1¼ hours, adding more broth if necessary. Remove from pan, let stand on a plate 15 minutes; reserve cooking liquid.

To serve, untie and loosen cheesecloth. Place serving platter over cabbage and quickly turn upside down. Overlap several of the largest reserved cabbage leaves on the top, so that the stuffed cabbage resembles a whole, uncooked cabbage. Use remaining leaves to circle platter. Serve Mushroom Sauce separately.

MUSHROOM SAUCE   about 2½ cups

¼ cup butter or margarine	1 teaspoon salt
½ pound mushrooms, sliced	¼ teaspoon white pepper
¼ cup all-purpose flour	2 cups cabbage cooking liquid

In a medium saucepan, melt butter; add mushrooms and sauté 5 minutes. Add flour, salt, and pepper; cook, stirring, 1 minute. Slowly stir in cooking liquid to make a smooth sauce. Cook, stirring constantly, until mixture thickens and is bubbly, about 5 minutes.

"Come for dessert and coffee"

This is the great way to entertain for a woman who likes to cook but who would just as soon skip the last-minute hassle of serving drinks and appetizers, then getting a complete dinner on the table.

A dessert buffet can be as simple or as elaborate as you want it to be. There should always be coffee, lots of it, and if you like, also offer a dessert wine. The simplest combination would be a fruit and cheese platter (see Index) and a plate of party cookies of several kinds (see Index). Or steer a middle course with a fruit/cheese combination of some kind, a custardy dessert, such as Crème Brûlée, and one "production" cake or pastry. Or be a show-off with fruit and cheese and nuts, plus several really spectacular desserts such as Bûche au Chocolat or Kransekake or Croquembouche or Spanish Windtorte or Dacquoise or Chocolate Treasure, so that guests can browse and taste and exclaim and enjoy— and complain to their heart's content about the weight that they are gaining.

Here are recipes for some of these gustatory delights. You can find many more of the same elegant sort in standard and specialty cookbooks. To begin with, an attractive cheese—fruit platter.

Brie with grapes, apples, and nuts: Slice about 2¼ pounds of seedless green grapes in half crosswise. Center a brie cheese that weighs about 2 pounds on a serving dish. Starting at the center, and moving round and round in a spiral, completely cover the top of the brie with the grape halves. Surround the cheese with unpeeled apple wedges, walnuts (cracked but not shelled), and wholegrain crackers.

A Bûche au Chocolat (chocolate log) is a splendid addition to any dessert-lover's culinary repertoire, for it will be welcome at any time of the year, is particularly appropriate at Christmas (Bûche de Noël), and can reappear again in February as a Lincoln's Log. If you're serving a crowd, butt two logs together and frost as one. The cake here is the classic génoise. The Italian Meringue, with slight variations, is used for filling and frosting and the "mushrooms" that decorate the log.

BUCHE AU CHOCOLAT

4 *large eggs, at room temperature*
⅔ *cup granulated sugar*
2 *teaspoons vanilla extract*
1 *lemon peel, grated*
½ *cup plus 2 tablespoons unsalted*
   butter

⅔ *cup plus 1 tablespoon*
   all-purpose flour, divided
⅓ *cup cake flour*
Confectioners sugar
Italian Meringue for filling, frosting,
   and decoration (recipes follow)

Preheat oven to 325°F. Place eggs in the large bowl of an electric mixer; gradually add granulated sugar, a small amount at a time, beating at low speed. Add vanilla and lemon peel; beat at high speed until eggs have doubled in volume and are thick, at least 5 minutes. Meanwhile, cut butter into small pieces; cook in a small saucepan, over moderate heat, until melted and very lightly browned. Remove from heat. Measure 2 tablespoons of the butter and combine with 1 tablespoon all-purpose flour. Line a 12- x 16-inch jelly roll pan with waxed paper, allowing the paper to hang over the ends. Using a pastry brush, paint the paper and the sides of the pan with the butter–flour mixture. Combine remaining ⅔ cup all-purpose flour and cake flour in a sifter. Sift about one-third over egg mixture; fold in. Add alternate small amounts of lukewarm butter and flour, folding lightly, until all flour and butter are used. Spread the batter in the prepared pan; bake 12 to 15 minutes, or until the top is lightly springy when touched and has just begun to brown. Remove from oven and sprinkle top evenly with confectioners sugar. Cover with waxed paper, then with a damp towel. Place a baking sheet on top of pan and turn over. Cool ten minutes; gently remove pan and peel off paper.

ITALIAN MERINGUE

3 *egg whites, at room temperature*
⅛ *teaspoon salt*

¼ *teaspoon cream of tartar*
1⅓ *cups sugar*

Place egg whites in the large mixer bowl; beat at low speed until foamy. Add salt and cream of tartar; beat at high speed until stiff peaks form. Place sugar in a small saucepan; add ½ cup water. Place over high heat, swirling pan gently until sugar is dissolved. Cover pan; boil rapidly (do not stir) until mixture begins to thicken; remove cover and bring to 238°F. on candy thermometer (soft-ball stage). Turn mixer speed to medium; pour sugar syrup into egg whites in a thin stream, continuing to beat. Turn speed to high and beat until mixture is cool, about 5 minutes.

To make mushrooms: Preheat oven to 200°F. Butter and flour a baking sheet. Place about ¼ of the meringue mixture into a pastry bag fitted with a plain tube about ½ inch in diameter. Press out rounded domes about 1 inch in diameter (for the mushroom tops) on baking sheet.

Press out small, upright cones (for stems) separately. You will need only 5 or 6 mushrooms. Bake about 1 hour, or until they lift easily from baking sheet.

filling and frosting:

12 ounces semisweet chocolate

⅓ cup strong coffee

1 teaspoon vanilla extract

½ cup unsalted butter, softened, divided

3 tablespoons unsweetened cocoa

½ cup (about) confectioners sugar

In a small, heavy saucepan, over moderate heat, melt the chocolate in the coffee. Cool slightly; beat into remaining meringue along with vanilla and ¼ cup butter. Remove about two-thirds of the mixture and reserve. Into remaining meringue mixture, beat remaining ¼ cup butter. Spread this filling over the sheet of cake. Roll up, jelly-roll fashion, starting at one long side. Place on serving dish. Beat cocoa into reserved meringue mixture. (If too soft to spread, refrigerate for a short time.) Use to frost the roll. Draw the tines of a fork through the frosting to simulate the bark of a tree. Using a small knife, make a hole in the underside of each mushroom cap; fill with a dab of frosting and insert a stem. Repeat with remaining mushrooms; arrange mushrooms on top of log. Sprinkle confectioners sugar lightly over all.

Chocolate Treasure is a wickedly delicious concoction, a sort of rich-uncle relative of old-fashioned icebox cake. Its base is the same cake used for Bûche au Chocolat.

CHOCOLATE TREASURE   16 servings

cake:

Two recipes of génoise, as for Bûche au Chocolat; make two single recipes, baking each batter separately, rather than doubling the recipe.

filling:

1½ pounds (24 squares) semisweet chocolate

½ cup strong coffee, at room temperature

½ cup grand marnier liqueur

3 egg yolks

1 cup egg whites (from 6 to 9 eggs)

⅛ teaspoon salt

¼ cup sugar

1 cup heavy cream

Melt chocolate in double boiler over hot water. Scrape into the small bowl of an electric mixer and let stand until it reaches room temperature. At lowest speed of mixer, beat coffee and grand marnier into chocolate, scraping bowl often; beat in egg yolks, scraping bowl, only until mixture is smooth. In the large bowl of the electric mixer, beat the egg whites and salt until soft peaks form. Gradually beat in sugar; continue to beat until stiff but not dry. Fold 2 heaping tablespoons of egg whites, one at a time, into chocolate mixture. Fold in half of remaining whites, then fold chocolate mixture into remaining whites, continuing to fold until no streaks of whites show. Beat cream until it holds soft peaks. Fold into chocolate mixture.

To assemble the cake: Using the base of a 9- x 3-inch springform pan as a pattern, cut one circle from each sheet of cake, positioning the pattern as far into one corner as possible. Put pan together; line bottom with waxed paper. Place one circle of cake in bottom of pan; reserve second circle. From remaining cake, cut 3-inch-high strips; use to line the sides of the pan, pressing cake together wherever it meets to make a tight fit. Pour the filling into the cake-lined pan. Fit the second cake circle on top, trimming the lining with scissors if the filling does not reach the top. Cover with foil or plastic wrap and place a light weight on the top (a baking sheet or cake pan with a can of canned food placed on top will do nicely). Refrigerate overnight; or, if you wish, the cake may be frozen at this point. Make the chocolate glaze and English custard sauce in the morning of the day on which the cake is to be served.

Chocolate glaze: Break 6 ounces of semisweet chocolate into a small, heavy saucepan. Add ½ cup of boiling water. Stir chocolate over low heat until it is smooth. Remove it from the heat and allow it to cool to room temperature.

English custard sauce: In a heavy saucepan, over moderate heat, scald 1 cup of milk and 1 cup of heavy cream. Place 4 egg yolks in the top of a double boiler; stir lightly, just to mix. Whisk in ½ cup of sugar and ⅛ teaspoon of salt. Very slowly whisk in scalded milk. Place the mixture over simmering water. Cook the mixture, stirring constantly, until it thickens slightly and will coat a metal spoon. Remove it from the heat; strain it and stir in 1 teaspoon of vanilla extract or 1 tablespoon of grand marnier.

To finish the dessert: Remove the sides of the springform pan. Place a serving plate on top of the dessert and invert it very carefully. Gently remove the bottom of the pan and peel off the waxed paper. Cut strips of waxed paper and gently tuck them under the cake to protect the plate. Working quickly, pour the chocolate glaze over the cake, allowing a small amount to run down the sides; using a metal spatula, spread the glaze smoothly on the sides of the cake. Refrigerate the cake until serving time. Serve the custard sauce separately, for guests to use or not, as they desire.

Reluctantly turning away from chocolate for a moment, consider Spanish Windtorte, which doesn't come from Spain but from Vienna, whose master bakers like, for some reason, to give their most elegant creations Spanish names. This is an exceedingly handsome, crisp, airy meringue shell with a fruit-and-cream filling; it serves particularly well as a companion piece to Bûche au Chocolat or Chocolate Treasure. Make the shell of the torte the day before you plan to serve it.

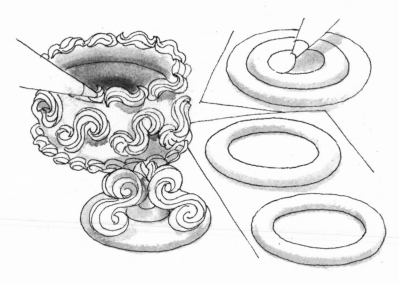

SPANISH WINDTORTE   12 servings

7 egg whites, divided
½ teaspoon cream of tartar,
   divided

1¾ cup sugar, divided
Fruit Filling (recipe follows)

Line two baking sheets with unglazed brown wrapping paper. On one, draw two 8-inch circles (use 8-inch cake pan for pattern); on second pan, draw one circle. Preheat oven to 225°F. In mixer bowl, beat 3 egg whites with ¼ teaspoon cream of tartar until soft peaks form. Little by little, sprinkle in ¾ cup sugar, continuing to beat at high speed until sugar is dissolved and mixture forms stiff peaks. Spoon into a pastry bag fitted with a #5 star tube. Just inside one circle on baking sheet, pipe a ring of meringue; continue in a spiral, piping concentric, touching rings to entirely fill the circle. This will be the base of the torte. Just inside each of the other two circles, pipe a single ring of meringue about ¾-inch wide. Use any leftover meringue to make these two circles higher. Bake 45 minutes; turn oven off, leave meringues in oven, with door closed, 45 minutes longer. Peel off paper; cool meringues on racks. (Work gently— they are fragile.) Beat remaining egg whites, cream of tartar, and sugar in the same manner as before. Line a baking sheet with fresh brown paper. Place cooled meringue layer on paper; stack the two circles of

177

meringue on top of it, using some of the new, unbaked meringue as adhesive to hold them together. Frost outside of shell with a thin, smooth layer of the new meringue. Place remaining new meringue in pastry bag; pipe decorative border around top and bottom edges of shell, and decorate sides with swirls of meringue. Preheat oven to 225°F. On another piece of brown paper, draw a 6-inch circle. Fill in, about ¾ inch deep, with meringue; pipe a decorative border on the edge; this piece will be the cover of the torte. Also pipe three S-shapes, about 3 inches long, at the other end of the paper. Reserve remaining meringue (you will need only about 1 tablespoon). Bake 30 minutes; turn off heat and leave in oven, with door closed, overnight. In the morning, remove the S-shapes from paper, lean them against one another, standing up, and fasten them with a little of the leftover meringue. Fasten to the top of the torte cover with the remaining meringue. Store all in a dry place; do not refrigerate. Just before serving, place shell on serving plate, spoon filling into hollow center, and top with torte cover.

FRUIT FILLING

2 cups heavy cream
2 tablespoons confectioners
    sugar
1 tablespoon vanilla extract
2 (10-ounce) packages frozen
    peaches, partially thawed

1 (10-ounce) packaged frozen
    raspberries, partially thawed
1 cup fresh or thawed frozen
    blueberries

Whip cream with sugar and vanilla until stiff. Drain fruits, reserving a few perfect pieces for decoration. Layer fruits with cream in meringue shell, drizzling a little juice over each fruit layer. Decorate meringue cover with reserved fruit pieces; serve immediately.

Still in the meringue department, here is Dacquoise, a meringue torte made with ground nuts and put together with a smooth, coffee-flavored butter-cream filling.

DACQUOISE   10 to 12 servings

⅝ cup toasted almonds, ground
⅝ cup toasted filberts, ground
¾ cup plus 2½ tablespoons
    granulated sugar, divided
1 tablespoon cornstarch
6 egg whites

⅛ teaspoon salt
¼ teaspoon cream of tartar
1 teaspoon vanilla extract
¼ teaspoon almond extract
Coffee Butter Cream (recipe follows)
Confectioners sugar

On three baking sheets, place unglazed brown paper or parchment paper. On each, draw a 10-inch circle. Preheat oven to 275°F. In a bowl, combine the ground almonds and filberts with ¾ cup sugar; sift the cornstarch over them. Mix well, making certain there are no lumps; set aside. In large mixer bowl, beat egg whites until foamy; add salt and cream of tartar, beat until soft peaks form. At highest speed, beat in remaining sugar, and the vanilla and almond extracts. Fold in nut mixture by hand. Place in a pastry bag fitted with a plain #5 tube. Just inside each of the 10-inch circles on paper, pipe two touching rounds of the nut meringue. Then, starting from center and working out, fill in each circle with concentric, touching rounds to make complete layers. Smooth each gently with a spatula. Bake 1 hour, or until meringue feels firm to the touch. Cool a few moments, peel off paper. Place one layer on serving plate, spread with Coffee Butter Cream. Top with second layer, cover with butter cream; top with third layer. Use remaining butter cream to frost sides of cake, first trimming the edges of the layers (with scissors), if necessary, to provide a smooth surface. Sprinkle top of cake with confectioners sugar. Refrigerate until serving time.

COFFEE BUTTER CREAM

⅔ cup sugar
⅛ teaspoon cream of tartar
1½ tablespoons instant espresso
  coffee powder

6 egg yolks
1 cup unsalted butter, softened

Place sugar, cream of tartar, coffee powder, and ⅓ cup of water in a small, heavy saucepan. Stir over moderate heat until sugar is dissolved. Cover pan; bring to a boil. Uncover; without stirring, allow mixture to come to 236°F. on candy thermometer. In a bowl, beat egg yolks until thick. Add sugar mixture in a thin stream, beating constantly; continue to beat until completely cool. Beat in butter, 1 tablespoon at a time. Cover and refrigerate 30 minutes before using.

Croquembouche, a piled-high tower of tiny cream puffs held together with a caramel glaze, is a treat for the eye and the sweet tooth. It's a dessert that looks infinitely more difficult to make than it really is. The first requirement is time, the second patience. Make the puffs (pâte à chou) and the filling (crème pâtissière) the day before you plan on serving the dessert; assemble the Croquembouche the morning of the party.

CROQUEMBOUCHE   15 to 20 servings

pâte à chou:
¾ cup butter
1½ cups all-purpose flour

⅛ teaspoon salt
6 eggs

Preheat oven to 375°F. Place the butter, with 1½ cups water, in a saucepan; bring to a boil. Add the flour and salt all at once; beat until mixture forms a ball and leaves the sides of the pan. Add the eggs one at a time, beating the mixture smooth after each addition. Drop by rounded teaspoonfuls, 2 inches apart, onto greased baking sheets. Bake 30 to 35 minutes, or until puffed and golden brown. (They must be crisp.) Cool on wire racks. Using a pointed knife, make a small hole in the bottom of each puff. Store loosely covered. You should have about 90 puffs.

crème pâtissière:

3 cups milk	½ cup all-purpose flour
8 egg yolks	⅛ teaspoon salt
1 cup sugar	1 teaspoon vanilla extract

Scald the milk. Place egg yolks and sugar in the top of a double boiler and beat until fluffy. Add flour and salt slowly, stirring until smooth. Add the scalded milk very slowly, stirring constantly. Place over boiling water and continue to stir until smooth and thick. Remove from heat; stir in vanilla. Place a piece of plastic wrap directly on the surface to cover. Refrigerate.

Fill the puffs: Spoon the chilled crème pâtissière into a pastry bag fitted with a plain #4 tube. Fill each puff by inserting the tube into the hole made in the bottom. Refrigerate the filled puffs in a single layer.

Prepare your equipment: Cut a 9-inch circle from a piece of heavy cardboard; cover it smoothly with foil. Set the circle on a larger piece of foil near the stove so that you can work quickly in assembling the Croquembouche. Lay out two table forks and a pair of tongs. Make the caramel dip for the puffs.

Caramel dip: Place 2 cups of sugar, ½ teaspoon of cream of tartar, and 1½ cups of water in a heavy skillet. Bring the mixture to a boil, stirring until the sugar is dissolved. Reduce the heat and cook the mixture until the syrup is a pale amber color. Lower the heat so that the mixture barely simmers.

Assemble the Croquembouche: Lightly dip one side of a puff into caramel and place at the outer edge of the foil-covered circle, caramel side down and top facing outward. Repeat all around the circle, letting the edges of the puffs touch. (The caramel will harden, making the puffs adhere to the foil and to one another.) Repeat, making a second row of puffs positioned between and on top of those of the first row (let them lean a little toward the inside). Fill in the center, behind the circles of puffs, with more puffs to make a solid layer. Continue making circles, each a little smaller than the last, and filling in behind the circles, to form a cone-shape. Top the Croquembouche with a single puff. If the caramel becomes too thick before you are finished, add a little hot water to it and bring it again to simmering. Make sure that the syrup does not burn. Refrigerate the finished Croquembouche, uncovered.

Opposite: For dessert and coffee—Croquembouche and a fruit-and-cheese platter

Add 1 cup of water and ½ teaspoon of butter to the caramel remaining in the skillet. Cook the mixture, stirring occasionally, to 232°F. on a candy thermometer. Pour it into a small bowl and store it at room temperature.

To serve: Remove the Croquembouche from the refrigerator. Leaving it on its foil-covered cardboard, place it on a serving plate. Protect the plate with strips of waxed paper. Drizzle the reserved caramel syrup over the dessert. If you wish, sift confectioners sugar lightly over the caramel. Remove the waxed paper and circle the Croquembouche with fresh leaves or with leaves and flowers. Let guests serve themselves from the Croquembouche pyramid, starting at the top, using two forks or serving tongs. As a final topping, provide whipped cream.

Another sort of pyramid, equally eye-filling and mouth-watering, is Kransekake, a Scandinavian creation served on special occasions, made up of crunchy macaroonlike rings piled high and decorated with Royal Frosting.

KRANSEKAKE
20 to 24 servings

4 egg whites
4 (8-ounce) cans or packages
  almond paste

3 cups sifted confectioners sugar
Royal Frosting (recipe follows)

In the large bowl of an electric mixer, beat egg whites until foamy. Slowly crumble in almond paste, beating at low speed until all almond paste has been incorporated and mixture is smooth. Slowly add sugar, beating mixture until it is smooth and well blended. Using a pencil, draw 12 circles on unglazed brown wrapping paper or parchment paper. Make the largest 7½ inches in diameter and decrease the diameter of each subsequent circle by ½ inch (the smallest circle will have a diameter of 2 inches). Grease the papers well. Preheat oven to 300°F. Spoon almond mixture into a pastry bag without a tube; the bag should have an opening at the tip about 1 inch in diameter. Squeeze mixture into rings, just inside the pencil marks. With remaining mixture, make two S-shapes and a star to decorate the top of the pyramid. Slide papers onto baking sheets. Bake several at once, 25 to 30 minutes, or until golden. Remove rings carefully from papers, cool on racks. (Kransekake pans, ring-shaped, are available if you are not a lover of pastry bags. See Tools of the Trade.)

ROYAL FROSTING

3 egg whites
½ teaspoon cream of tartar

1 (1-pound) package confectioners
  sugar, sifted

In a mixer bowl, combine egg whites and cream of tartar; beat until foamy.

Slowly beat in confectioners sugar until well blended. At high speed, beat mixture until it holds its shape—until a knife drawn through it leaves a sharp, clean path. Cover with a damp towel to keep from hardening. May be tinted with food coloring, if desired.

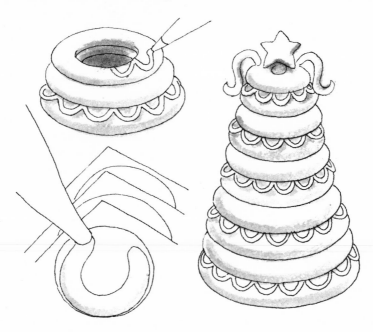

To assemble the Kransekake: Pipe Royal Frosting (using any plain tube) in wavy lines over every other ring. Starting with the largest ring, build a pyramid of graduated rings. Put the S-shapes and star on top, anchoring them with frosting. Use the remaining frosting to decorate the pyramid as you choose. To serve, remove one ring at a time, starting at the top, and break into serving pieces.

When you make one of these wonderful desserts that uses a large number of egg whites, you might as well make a companion piece that uses up the leftover yolks. Crème Brûlée is such a dessert—a Creole concoction of a velvety custard with a topping of broiled brown sugar.

CREME BRULEE 8 servings

8 egg yolks
¼ cup plus 2 tablespoons
    granulated sugar
4 cups heavy cream, scalded

2 teaspoons vanilla extract
Light brown sugar

Preheat oven to 350°F. In a bowl, stir egg yolks lightly, just enough to break and mix them. Add sugar to scalded cream; stir to dissolve. Very gradually, beginning a spoonful at a time, stir cream into yolks. Stir in vanilla. Pour into a flat, shallow 6-cup baking dish. Place dish in a larger baking pan; pour hot water into the larger pan to come halfway up the sides of the smaller dish. Bake about 30 minutes, or until a knife inserted in the center comes out clean. Remove from the hot water to a wire rack. Cool, then refrigerate at least 6 hours or overnight. Place about ¾ cup brown sugar in a small strainer. With the fingertips, press it through the strainer onto the custard in an even layer about ¼ inch thick. Pat very gently to make a smooth, even, compact layer. Broil about 8 inches below the source of heat until the sugar is completely melted—a matter of minutes. (Leave the broiler door ajar and don't take your eyes off it, as it burns readily.) Remove from broiler. Cool, then refrigerate 1 to 8 hours. To serve, crack the topping with a serving spoon and spoon into serving dishes, including some topping in each serving.

Fruit—whenever, wherever

Fruit is the favorite dessert of many people, particularly those not over-fond of sweets. A bowl or shallow compote of several kinds of fruit, buffed to a handsome shine, is pretty enough to centerpiece any kind of buffet table. But there may be times when you want, if not to improve on nature, at least to give her a helping hand. Here are three lovely fruit-dessert centerpieces that can serve you well as the focal point of any buffet-service meal, from brunch through dinner or an after-dinner dessert buffet.

SPARKLING FRUIT PYRAMID   about 15 servings

2 egg whites
Granulated sugar
7 red eating apples
5 medium navel oranges

3 comice or d'anjou pears
1 bunch red or purple grapes,
   separated into small clusters

In a medium bowl, beat egg whites with 1 teaspoon water just until mixed. Dip each piece of fruit into egg white and shake off excess; dip into sugar so that the fruit is lightly but evenly covered. Let stand on wire rack several hours, until coating is completely dry. Arrange apples in a circle on a serving dish. Make a smaller circle of oranges on top of apples; secure with small skewers or food picks. Top oranges with pears; fasten in the same manner. Tuck little clusters of grapes in the openings between fruit. Tuck fresh green leaves around the bottom of the pyramid.

PINEAPPLE BOATS WITH STRAWBERRIES   16 servings

4 small, ripe fresh pineapples
1 cup kirsch or pear brandy

48 whole fresh strawberries

Opposite: A fantasy of sweet decorations

Cut a slice from bottom of each pineapple; cut each pineapple into quarters lengthwise, cutting through both fruit and foliage. Using a very sharp knife, cut the core from each quarter; run knife between fruit and skin, loosening fruit but leaving it in place. Cut each quarter into 8 to 10 slices, cutting through fruit but not through skin. Sprinkle with kirsch. Refrigerate. Wash and hull strawberries. Slice thin lengthwise. Arrange slices, overlapping, into flower shapes on top of each pineapple quarter.

GOLDEN ORANGES   12 servings

1 dozen medium navel oranges   *¼ cup coarsely shredded orange*
4 cups sugar   *peel*
¼ cup light corn syrup   *Golden Sauce (recipe follows)*

Peel fruit, leaving fruit whole. Gently scrape off excess white membrane from oranges; carefully remove white center core. Separate sections very slightly at one end. If necessary, cut a thin slice from opposite end so that orange will stand up. In a heavy saucepan, combine sugar with 2 cups water; stir to dissolve. Bring to a boil; boil rapidly 6 to 7 minutes, until syrup is pale amber color. Remove from heat. Carefully (it will spatter) add corn syrup and orange peel and 2 additional cups water. Boil rapidly until slightly thickened, 8 to 10 minutes. Place oranges in a large, shallow serving bowl. Pour syrup immediately over oranges. Refrigerate at least 6 hours, basting frequently. Just before serving, tuck sprigs of mint around edge of bowl. Serve Golden Sauce separately.

GOLDEN SAUCE

2 cups sugar   *½ cup butter*
½ cup light corn syrup   *⅔ cup light cream*

In a heavy saucepan, cook sugar over medium heat, stirring frequently, until melted and golden brown. Remove from heat; blend in corn syrup, then butter. Add cream, a very little at a time, stirring until smooth. Serve at room temperature.

A gold star for the cook

Even if you aren't the greatest cook of the era, you can produce great party foods—which tend to make for great parties—if you plan in advance and cook in advance. Do all possible preparing before it's necessary to keep one eye on the clock. Never, never serve more than one dish that has to have anything (other than decorating or garnishing) done to it at the last minute. Nothing that has to be watched, or coddled, or stood over.

Tools of the Trade

Unless you really enjoy cooking, you would not be reading this book. And if you like to cook, it can be presupposed that your kitchen is already fitted with a full complement of the more usual cooking paraphernalia, including sharp knives of assorted sizes; a mixer and a blender; an assortment of pans for stove-top and oven cooking, including heavy saucepans and pots with well-fitting covers, a double boiler, baking pans of various sizes, and sheet, tube and layer cake pans; cups for dry and wet measuring, and measuring spoons; bowls and containers for mixing and storage; whisks and metal and wooden spoons, plain and slotted. You've probably acquired a number of cookery gadgets, too, some of which you wouldn't be without, some of which you never use.

If there are items mentioned in these pages that you don't have but want, they probably can be purchased at any store or large housewares department that specializes in high-quality cookware. Almost every city or town of any size has at least one such store. If you don't know its name and location, consult the classified section of your phone book under such headings as "cooking utensils," "housewares," and "gourmet shops."

Many of the things you want or need can be ordered by mail. There are a number of mail-order houses offering supplies of this kind, but first try either of the following two. They offer virtually everything you can possibly think of to use in food garnishing and decorating.

MAID OF SCANDINAVIA COMPANY
3244 Raleigh Avenue
Minneapolis, Minnesota 55416

WILTON ENTERPRISES, INC.
833 West 115th Street
Chicago, Illinois 60643

Maid of Scandinavia issues a yearly catalog in the autumn, plus winter and spring supplements containing new items. Wilton issues an annual Cake and Food Decorating Yearbook that contains, in addition to a listing of all the items offered for sale, mini-lessons in decorating techniques and ideas for food decorating and garnishing. There is a charge for the catalogs of both firms; Maid of Scandinavia credits the price of the catalog on orders above a specified amount.

What can you buy by mail? Almost anything connected with garnishing and decorating. Just browsing through the catalogs is a decorating education. You'll find yourself saying again and again, "I didn't know there was such a thing!"as you come across one ingenious, helpful gadget after another. (And, perhaps, as happens with almost all catalogs, you may say also, "Who on earth would want a thing like that!" But to each his own.)

Whatever you want or need or just plain covet, you'll find it in one or the other of the catalogs, or in both. Pots and pans of all sizes and shapes, including an amazing array of shape and form pans and molds of all descriptions. Frosting, filling, and cake mixes; sprinkles, colored sugars, and other edible decorations; paste and liquid food coloring in a rainbow of colors; flavoring extracts of many kinds; decorating bags and parchment papers; all the many shapes and sizes of decorating tubes. Cutters of every imaginable shape, size from minuscule to enormous Cookbooks and books on specific techniques of various phases of decorating and garnishing for beginning, advanced, and professional decorators. Candy molds, sugar molds, and chocolate molds. Nonedible decorations and party favors. Cookery tools of all sorts. Gadgets galore. Have fun!

Index